MW01697749

Planning, Writing, and Implementing

IEPs

A Christian Approach

Second Edition

Dr. Bunnie Claxton

Liberty University

Kendall Hunt

publishing company

Kendall Hunt
publishing company

www.kendallhunt.com
Send all inquiries to:
4050 Westmark Drive
Dubuque, IA 52004-1840

PAK ISBN: 978-1-7924-8164-2
Text ISBN: 978-1-7924-8163-5

Published in the United States of America

Contents

Preface

What makes *Planning, Writing, and Implementing IEPs: A Christian Approach* different from other IEP books on the market? First this book goes far beyond completing paperwork and conducting meetings, and addresses the comprehensive nature of the IEP process. More importantly, this book approaches the IEP process from a Christian perspective reminding the reader to look at each IEP as an opportunity to serve a family by providing hope and a vision for the student's education. Throughout this book, teachers, administrators, service providers, and parents, are challenged to consider an IEP from a different perspective. This book reminds readers that IEP meetings need not be a time of conflict and controversy, and that writing the components of an IEP can become part of a plan for the student's future (Jeremiah 29:11), rather than a dreaded task to complete. The book is written from the perspective of an educator with over 25 years of experience working with students receiving various levels of special education services. The Bible is the most often referenced book. It is this perspective that makes this book unique.

Acknowledgments

I want to thank several people for making this book possible. First, I want to thank the Lord Jesus Christ for presenting me with this opportunity and for giving me the words and wisdom needed to write it. Apart from Him, this book would not exist. I would also like to thank my husband, Dr. Russ Claxton, for his support as I wrote this book on planes, trains, and automobiles over several holidays and vacations, as well as many early mornings, late evenings, and weekends. Thank you for supporting me though this journey! Curtis and Amanda, from Kendall Hunt publishing, you were incredible to work with, and I hope we are able to work together again in the future. Thank you for late nights and hard deadlines that we always met or beat! To my amazing friend, Carol Dolan, who is always there for me to lend her encouragement and wisdom in time of need. Thank you for being an amazing friend and prayer warrior. To Dr. Deanna Keith for supporting me from the very beginning and for participating on such a personal and emotional level in this project. You are a dear, dear friend, and I am so thankful to have you in my life! Thank you, also to Dr. Jennifer Landrum and Dr. Megan Cordes for saying, "yes." I am forever grateful to you both for your belief in a book about IEPs written from a Christian perspective! I feel blessed beyond measure!

About the Author

Photo courtesy of Lee Claxton

Dr. Bunnie L. Claxton, Ed.D. is the Director of Applied Research at Liberty University. She is an associate professor at Liberty University and an adjunct instructor at Colorado Christian University. She has 25 years of experience in the field of education, including public, private, homeschool, and higher education. She has developed multiple graduate level courses, chaired dissertations, served as a research methodologist, subject matter expert, and instructional mentor to professors. Her scholarly publications include *A Step-by-Step Guide to Applied Research in Education*, *A Step-by-Step Guide to Qualitative Research in Education*, *A Step-by-Step Guide to Quantitative Research in Education*, A Step-By-Step Guide to Writing a Literature Review in Doctoral Research, *Planning, Writing, and Implementing IEPs: A Christian Approach*, and she also served as a contributing author for two additional books. Dr. Claxton served as the Superintendent for Liberty University Online Academy, an online K-12 school with over 6,000 students.

IEP: Documents & Details Essential for a Quality Individual Education Program

Liberty Academic School

Documents & Details Essential for a Quality Individual Education Program

Liberty Academic School
XXXX XXXX XXXXXX
XXXXXXX XXXXXX
XXXXXXX XXXXXX
Telephone: XXXXXX
Fax: XXXXXXXXXX
Email: xxxxx@xxxx.com
Website: www.xxxxxxx.com

Individualized Education Plan
Meeting Notice

Name: ____________________ Date: ____________________

You are invited to attend an IEP meeting for your child: ____________________

Meeting Details:

Date: ________

Time: ________

Location: _____

Purpose of Meeting:

_____ IEP Development
_____ IEP Review
_____ Discuss Services[1]
_____ Transition[2]
_____ Manifestation Determination
_____ Other

[1]If the purpose of this meeting is to discuss services, service personnel may be invited.

[2]If the purpose of the meeting is to discuss transition, the student will be invited.

If you are unable to attend the meeting at this scheduled time and location, or if you would like additional information prior to the meeting, please contact the IEP team leader below to reschedule.

_______________ _______________ _______________

Team Leader Email Phone Number

Participants Involved:
Below is a list of participants invited to this IEP meeting. Attendance is required.

Name of Participant	Position

Individualized Education Plan
Meeting Notice, continued

Please keep the first page, and return this page to the team leader.

________________	________________________	________________
Team Leader	Email	Phone Number

Meeting Details:

Date: _________

Time: ________

Location: _____

Based on the date and location above:

_____ I WILL attend the IEP meeting as scheduled

_____ I WILL NOT attend the IEP meeting as scheduled

If you will not attend the meeting. Please complete the following:

_____ Please contact me to reschedule the meeting.

_____ I can participate via WebEx or ________________

_____ Please hold the meeting without me.

_____ I give permission to proceed without a meeting.

_____ If no response, proceed with meeting.

_____ I would like to share my input via other means (email, telephone, mail).

_________________	_____________
Signature of Parent	Date

Liberty Academic School
XXXX XXXX XXXXXX
XXXXXXX XXXXXX
XXXXXXX XXXXXX
Telephone: XXXXXX
Fax: XXXXXXXXXX
Email: xxxxx@xxxx.com
Website: www.xxxxxxx.com

Individualized Education Plan
Team Member Excusal Request

If the team member's area of curriculum, related services, or expertise will be discussed, the team member may be excused, but must provide written comments and submit for approval 10 days prior to the meeting. If the team members' area of curriculum, related services, or expertise will not be discussed the team member may be excused without written documentation.

The following team members have requested to be excused from the meeting.

Name of Participant	Position	Reason

The excusal request is for the following date:

Student Name: _______________

IEP Meeting Date: ______________________

Meeting Location: ______________________

___ **I agree to excuse the above team member from the meeting.**

____
Signature of Parent

____
Date

____
Signature of Administrator/District Representative

____
Date

Liberty Academic School
Liberty Academic School
XXXX XXXX XXXXXX
XXXXXXX XXXXXX
XXXXXXX XXXXXX
Telephone: XXXXXX
Fax: XXXXXXXXXX
Email: xxxxx@xxxx.com
Website: www.xxxxxxx.com

Individualized Education Plan
Cover Page

Student Name: ______________________________ Date: ______________

Disability: ____

Grade: ______________ DOB: ____________ Age: ________

Parent/Guardian Name: __________________________

Street Address: ____

City: ____________________ State: ____________________ Zip Code: ______________

Phone #: ______________________

A copy of the IEP was given to the parent/guardian/student by: ______________________________

IEP Team Leader: ____ Phone #: ______________________

The Individualized Education Plan (IEP) that accompanies this document is meant to support the positive process and team approach. The IEP is a working document that outlines the vision for the student's future and includes the student's strengths and needs.

IEP Summary Information	
Projected IEP Start Date:	
Projected IEP End Date:	
Projected Annual Review Date:	
Projected Date for Reevaluation:	
Extended School Services	
Behavior Intervention Plan	
Supplementary Aids and Services	
Assistive Technology	
Supports for School Personnel	
Testing Accommodations	
Participate in State/District Assessments	
Special Transportation	

Participants Involved

The list below indicates that the individual participated in the development of the IEP and the decisions regarding placement. Participation does not authorize consent. Parent consent (or student if 18+ years of age) is indicated on the "Prior Notice" page.

Name of Participant	Position

Liberty Academic School
XXXX XXXX XXXXXX
XXXXXXX XXXXXX
XXXXXXX XXXXXX
Telephone: XXXXXX
Fax: XXXXXXXXXX
Email: xxxxx@xxxx.com
Website: www.xxxxxxx.com

Individualized Education Plan
Summary of Performance
Factors for IEP Team Consideration

Student Name: ______________________________ Date: ____________________

Disability: ____

DOB: _______________ Age: _______ Grade: ________

IEP Team Manager: __________________

The following information should be considered by the IEP team in regards to educational decisions made for the student, as it serves as a summary of the student's performance. Please see other sections of the IEP, as noted, for more precise details concerning specific areas of learning for this student.

1. Summary of Academic Achievement:

Include results of the initial or most recent evaluation of this student.

2. Strengths of the student:

3. Summary of Functional Performance, as applicable:

4. Summary of Transition: Postsecondary Goals, as applicable:

5. Parental concerns for enhancing the student's education:

6. Communication needs of the student:

7. Need for benchmarks or short-term objectives:

8. **Does the student require an Assistive Technology device and/or service?**

   Yes or No (circle one)

   If yes, does the committee recommend the device(s) be used in the student's home?

   Yes or No (circle one)

9. **Does the student need strategies, including behavioral interventions, supports, and other strategies to address behaviors that impede the student's learning or that of others?**

   Yes or No (circle one)

   If yes, does the student need a behavioral intervention plan?

   Yes or No (circle one)

10. **In the case of a student with limited English proficiency, does he/she need special education services to address his/her language needs as they relate to the IEP?**

    Yes or No or Not Applicable (circle one)

11. **In the case of a student who is blind or is visually impaired, the IEP team must provide for instruction or use of Braille if assessment results indicate need. When considering that Braille is not appropriate for the child, the IEP team may use the Functional Vision and Learning Media Assessment for Students who are Pre-Academic or Academic and Visually Impaired in Grades K-12 (FVLMA) or similar instrument.**

    Does this student need instruction in Braille or use of Braille?

    Yes or No or Not Applicable (circle one)

12. **In the case of a student who is deaf or hard of hearing, consider the student's language and communication needs, opportunities for direct communications with peers and professional personnel in the student's language and communication mode, academic level, and full range of needs, including opportunities for direct instruction in the student's language and communication mode.**

    Does this student need a particular device or service to address his/her communication needs?

    Yes or No or Not Applicable (circle one)

13. **Extended School Year (ESY)**

    Does this student require extended school year services?

    Yes or No (circle one)

Liberty Academic School

Liberty Academic School
XXXX XXXX XXXXXX
XXXXXXX XXXXXX
XXXXXXX XXXXXX

Telephone: XXXXXX
Fax: XXXXXXXXXX
Email: xxxxx@xxxx.com
Website: www.xxxxxxx.com

Individualized Education Plan
Present Level of Academic Achievement and Functional Performance (PLAAFP)

Student Name: ___________________________ Meeting Date: ____________

Student Strengths, Preferences, and Interests:
Assessment/Evaluation Data:

Current Student Academic Performance:

Effects of Disability on General Curriculum:

Describe the effect of student needs on progress in the general curriculum or, for a preschool student, effect of student needs on participation in appropriate activities.

Current Student Functional Performance: Social Competence: Physical Development:
Based on Effects, Describe Deficits that Require Functional Support:

Liberty Academic School
XXXX XXXX XXXXXX
XXXXXXX XXXXXX
XXXXXXX XXXXXX
Telephone: XXXXXX
Fax: XXXXXXXXXX
Email: xxxxx@xxxx.com
Website: www.xxxxxxx.com

Individualized Education Plan
Measurable Annual Goals

Student Name: ______________________ Meeting Date: ___________

The following goals are recommended to enable the student to be involved in and progress in the general education curriculum, address other educational needs that result from the student's disability, and prepare the student to meet his or her post-high-school goals.

Annual Goal: One		
Goal:		
Standard of learning related to this goal:		
Progress toward this goal will be measured: (Check all that apply)		
___ Tests and Quizzes ___ Standardized Test ___ Norm Referenced Test ___ Other Assessment	___ Classwork ___ Projects ___ Homework ___ Participation	___ Written Report ___ Observation ___ Checklist ___ Other
Progress toward this goal will be reported:		
Short-Term Objectives or Benchmarks, if necessary: or circle if N/A		
Objective/Benchmark One: Assessment method:		
Objective/Benchmark Two: Assessment method:		
Objective/Benchmark Three: Assessment method:		

Annual Goal: Two		
Goal:		
Standard of learning related to this goal:		
Progress toward this goal will be measured: (Check all that apply)		
___ Tests and Quizzes ___ Standardized Test ___ Norm Referenced Test ___ Other Assessment	___ Classwork ___ Projects ___ Homework ___ Participation	___ Written Report ___ Observation ___ Checklist ___ Other
Progress toward this goal will be reported:		
Short Term Objectives or Benchmarks, if necessary: or circle if N/A		
Objective/Benchmark One: Assessment method:		
Objective/Benchmark Two: Assessment method:		
Objective/Benchmark Three: Assessment method:		

Annual Goal: Three		
Goal:		
Standard of learning related to this goal:		
Progress toward this goal will be measured: (Check all that apply)		
___ Tests and Quizzes ___ Standardized Test ___ Norm Referenced Test ___ Other Assessment	___ Classwork ___ Projects ___ Homework ___ Participation	___ Written Report ___ Observation ___ Checklist ___ Other
Progress toward this goal will be reported:		
Short-Term Objectives or Benchmarks, if necessary: or circle if N/A		
Objective/Benchmark One: Assessment method:		
Objective/Benchmark Two: Assessment method:		
Objective/Benchmark Three: Assessment method:		

Annual Goal: Four		
Goal:		
Standard of learning related to this goal:		
Progress toward this goal will be measured: (Check all that apply)		
___ Tests and Quizzes ___ Standardized Test ___ Norm Referenced Test ___ Other Assessment	___ Classwork ___ Projects ___ Homework ___ Participation	___ Written Report ___ Observation ___ Checklist ___ Other
Progress toward this goal will be reported:		
Short-Term Objectives or Benchmarks, if necessary: or circle if N/A		
Objective/Benchmark One: Assessment method:		
Objective/Benchmark Two: Assessment method:		
Objective/Benchmark Three: Assessment method:		

Annual Goal: Five		
Goal:		
Standard of learning related to this goal:		
Progress toward this goal will be measured: (Check all that apply)		
___ Tests and Quizzes ___ Standardized Test ___ Norm Referenced Test ___ Other Assessment	___ Classwork ___ Projects ___ Homework ___ Participation	___ Written Report ___ Observation ___ Checklist ___ Other
Progress toward this goal will be reported:		
Short-Term Objectives or Benchmarks, if necessary: or circle if N/A		
Objective/Benchmark One: Assessment method:		
Objective/Benchmark Two: Assessment method:		
Objective/Benchmark Three: Assessment method:		

Annual Goal: Six		
Goal:		
Standard of learning related to this goal:		
Progress toward this goal will be measured: (Check all that apply)		
___ Tests and Quizzes ___ Standardized Test ___ Norm Referenced Test ___ Other Assessment	___ Classwork ___ Projects ___ Homework ___ Participation	___ Written Report ___ Observation ___ Checklist ___ Other
Progress toward this goal will be reported:		
Short-Term Objectives or Benchmarks, if necessary: or circle if N/A		
Objective/Benchmark One: Assessment method:		
Objective/Benchmark Two: Assessment method:		
Objective/Benchmark Three: Assessment method:		

Annual Goal: Seven		
Goal:		
Standard of learning related to this goal:		
Progress toward this goal will be measured: (Check all that apply)		
___ Tests and Quizzes ___ Standardized Test ___ Norm Referenced Test ___ Other Assessment	___ Classwork ___ Projects ___ Homework ___ Participation	___ Written Report ___ Observation ___ Checklist ___ Other
Progress toward this goal will be reported:		
Short-Term Objectives or Benchmarks, if necessary: or circle if N/A		
Objective/Benchmark One: Assessment method:		
Objective/Benchmark Two: Assessment method:		
Objective/Benchmark Three: Assessment method:		

Annual Goal: Eight		
Goal:		
Standard of learning related to this goal:		
Progress toward this goal will be measured: (Check all that apply)		
___ Tests and Quizzes ___ Standardized Test ___ Norm Referenced Test ___ Other Assessment	___ Classwork ___ Projects ___ Homework ___ Participation	___ Written Report ___ Observation ___ Checklist ___ Other
Progress toward this goal will be reported:		
Short-Term Objectives or Benchmarks, if necessary: or circle if N/A		
Objective/Benchmark One: Assessment method:		
Objective/Benchmark Two: Assessment method:		
Objective/Benchmark Three: Assessment method:		
Reporting Progress:		
*Progress will be reported at least as often as students without disabilities. Identify when periodic reports on the student's progress toward meeting the annual goals will be provided to the student's parents:		

Liberty Academic School

Liberty Academic School
XXXX XXXX XXXXXX
XXXXXXX XXXXXX
XXXXXXX XXXXXX
Telephone: XXXXXX
Fax: XXXXXXXXXX
Email: xxxxx@xxxx.com
Website: www.xxxxxxx.com

Individualized Education Plan
Least Restrictive Environment
Accommodations/Modifications

Student Name: ______________________________ Meeting Date: __________________

This student will be provided access to the general education, special education, other school services and activities, and education-related settings:

______ With no accommodations/modifications

______ With accommodations/modifications as follows:

Accommodations/Modifications					
Accommodations/ Modifications	Delivery Recommendations	Least Restrictive Environment	Frequency	Duration	Services Begin

Liberty Academic School
Liberty Academic School
XXXX XXXX XXXXXX
XXXXXXX XXXXXX
XXXXXXX XXXXXX
Telephone: XXXXXX
Fax: XXXXXXXXXX
Email: xxxxx@xxxx.com
Website: www.xxxxxxx.com

Individualized Education Program
Related Services

	Related Services					
Service	Service Delivery Recommendations	Person Responsible	Instructional Setting	Frequency	Duration	Services Begin

~ Identify, if applicable, class size, language (if other than English), group or individual services, direct and/or indirect consultant teacher services, or other service delivery recommendations.

12-Month Service and/or Program

Student is eligible to receive special education services and/or program during July/August:
Yes or No (circle one)
If yes,
______ Student will receive the same special education program/services as recommended above.
OR
______ Student will receive the following special education program/services:

Special Education Program/Services	**Service Delivery Recommendations**	**Instructional Setting**	**Frequency**	**Duration**	**Services Begin**

Liberty Academic School

Liberty Academic School
XXXX XXXX XXXXXX
XXXXXXX XXXXXX
XXXXXXX XXXXXX
Telephone: XXXXXX
Fax: XXXXXXXXXX
Email: xxxxx@xxxx.com
Website: www.xxxxxxx.com

Individualized Education Plan
Assessments

Individual testing accommodations, specific to the student's disability and needs, to be used consistently by the student in the recommended educational program and in the administration of district-wide assessments of the student achievement and, in accordance with department policy, state assessments of student achievement as indicated below.

______ No testing accommodations are recommended OR

Testing Accommodation	Condition	Implementation Recommendations
Describe the type, length, and purpose of the test upon which the use of testing accommodations is conditioned, if applicable. Identify the amount of extended time, type of setting, etc., specific to testing accommodations, if applicable.		

Narrative Explanation of Assessment Decision

Participation in State and District-wide Assessments

______ The student will participate in the same state and district-wide assessments administered to the general education students.

______ The student will participate in an alternate assessment on a state or district-wide assessment of student achievement. If checked, identify the alternate assessment below.

____
Alternate Assessment

Note the reason the student will not participate in the same state and district-wide assessments administered to the general education students and why the specific alternative assessment is appropriate.

Liberty Academic School
XXXX XXXX XXXXXX
XXXXXXX XXXXXX
XXXXXXX XXXXXX
Telephone: XXXXXX
Fax: XXXXXXXXXX
Email: xxxxx@xxxx.com
Website: www.xxxxxxx.com

Individualized Education Plan
Transition Plan Cover Page

Student Name: ______________________________ Date: ________________

Disability: ________________________

Grade: _______________ DOB: _________ Age: ________

Parent/Guardian Name: ____________________

Street Address: ____

City: _____________________ State: __________________ Zip Code: _____________

Phone #: __________________

A copy of the IEP was given to the parent/guardian/student on: _____________________________

IEP Team Leader: ___________________________________ Phone #: _____________________

The Individualized Education Plan (IEP) that accompanies this document is meant to support the team approach to ensuring successful outcomes for the student. The IEP is a working document that outlines the student's strengths, needs, and vision for the future. The intent of an IEP is to bring together a team of people who understand and support the student in order to come to a consensus on a transition plan that is appropriate and effective for the student.

Important Details to Document	Date
Transition IEP will be reviewed no later than	
Parent notified of Transition Plan IEP Meeting	
Student notified of Transition Plan IEP Meeting (if applicable)	
Transition Plan IEP Meeting	
Most recent eligibility date	
Next Re-evaluation, including eligibility, must occur before	

Participants Involved

The list below indicates that the individual participated in the development of the IEP and the decisions regarding placement. Participation does not authorize consent. Parent consent (or student if 18+) is indicated on the "Prior Notice" page.

Name of Participant	Position

Individualized Education Plan
Transition Cover Page, continued

The parent and student must be notified at least one year prior to the student turning 18 that the IDEA procedural safeguards will transfer to the student at the age of 18. This notice must be accompanied by an explanation of those procedural safeguards. If applicable, sign below documenting notification.

Parent Signature: ______________________________

Student Signature: ______________________________

Date informed: ______________________________

IEP Team Member or Administrator Signature: ______________________

Diploma and Transition Status

Projected Graduation Date: ____________

Is the student projected to graduate/exit this school year? Yes or No (circle one)
If yes, inform the parents and student that a *Summary of Performance* will be provided prior to graduating/exiting school.

Will the student be graduating with a standard, technical, or higher-level diploma or exceeding the age of eligibility this year? Yes or No (circle one)
If yes, a *Summary of Performance* must be provided to the student prior to graduating or exceeding the age of eligibility.

This student is a candidate for:	
______ Advanced Studies Diploma	______ Modified Standard Diploma
______ Advanced Technical Diploma	______ Special Diploma
______ Standard Diploma	______ Certificate of Completion Program
______ Technical Diploma	______ General Education Diploma
______ General Achievement Diploma	______ Not discussed at this time

Liberty Academic School
XXXX XXXX XXXXXX
XXXXXXX XXXXXX
XXXXXXX XXXXXX

Telephone: XXXXXX
Fax: XXXXXXXXXX
Email: xxxxx@xxxx.com
Website: www.xxxxxxx.com

Individualized Education Plan
Transition Plan

Transition plans should begin no later than when the student is 16 years of age, or earlier if required by state law or if deemed necessary by the IEP team. The plan for transition services must be discussed and documented annually.

Student Name: ______________________________ Age: _____

Date Form Completed: ____

Anticipated Graduation Date: ____

Current IEP Dates from: ____________ to: ____________

Post-Secondary Goal

In the box below, write the student's post-secondary goal. This goal should be written in collaboration with the IEP team including the family and student. Include preferences, interests, and desired outcomes for post-secondary education, training, employment, and adult living.

In the box below, write the disability-related skills that require IEP goals and/or related services. Consider all disability-related skills necessary for the student to achieve the stated post-secondary vision noted above.

Individualized Education Plan
Transition Plan, continued

Transition Plan Activities		
Needed Activities to Facilitate the Student's Movement from School to Post-School Activities	**Service/Activity**	**School/District/Agency Responsible**

Liberty Academic School

Liberty Academic School
XXXX XXXX XXXXXX
XXXXXXX XXXXXX
XXXXXXX XXXXXX
Telephone: XXXXXX
Fax: XXXXXXXXXX
Email: xxxxx@xxxx.com
Website: www.xxxxxxx.com

Individualized Education Plan
Prior Notice and Parental Consent

Student Name:_________________________________

Meeting Details:

IEP Meeting Date: ___________________

Meeting Time: _______________________

Meeting Location: ____________________

Please complete and return this form to:

______________	________________________	_________________
Team Leader	Email	Phone Number

This document serves as notice prior to implementing this IEP. The decisions made in this IEP are based on a review of the students Present Levels of Academic and Functional Achievement. Relevant documentation to these decisions, if any, are attached. If you need additional information or have concerns, please contact the team leader.

Parent/Adult Student Consent: Indicate your decision by checking the appropriate space below and sign.

______ I GIVE permission to implement this IEP.

______ I DO NOT GIVE permission to implement this IEP.

____ ___________

Parent or Adult Student Signature Date

Transfer of Rights at the Age of Majority (age 18)

Indicate the date that the student and parent were informed of the transfer of parental rights under IDEA to the adult student at the age of 18. This must occur at least one year prior to the student turning 18 years of age.

I was informed of the parental rights under IDEA and that these rights transfer to me at age 18.

____ ___________

Adult Student Signature Date

I was informed of the parental rights under IDEA that transfer to my child at age 18.

____ ___________

Parent Signature Date

Functional Behavior Assessment Summary

Student: ______________________ DOB: _________________________
School: _______________________ Grade: ________________________
Date: _________________________ Assessor: _____________________

Data Sources:

- ☐ Observations (settings: classroom, lunchroom)
- ☐ Teacher interview
- ☐ Student interview
- ☐ Parent contact
- ☐ Other____________

Description of Behaviors: (use concrete terms, provide specific descriptors of behaviors)

Frequency of Behaviors:

Duration of Behaviors:

Intensity: (Impact of the target behavior on students, peers, and the learning environment)

Setting: (Where does the behavior occur? Include time of day, with specific individuals, structured or unstructured setting, etc.)

Triggers: (Identify circumstances that appear to begin the behavior.)

Consequences: (what is the response after the behavior has occurred?)

Educational Impact: (How does the behavior impact learning for self and others?)

Strengths/Resources

Student:

School:

Family:

Community:

Function of the Student's Behavior: (What purpose does the behavior serve for the student?)

- ☐ To regulate affect (i.e., anxiety, anger, depression, lack of self-esteem)
- ☐ To gain attention
- ☐ To gain control
- ☐ To avoid/escape settings, tasks, individuals, situations
- ☐ To obtain specific object or activities
- ☐ To avoid/escape internal distractions (psychological/physical/neurological difficulties)
- ☐ To communicate needs or desires (lacks effective communication skills)
- ☐ Other ____________

Observational Data:

Hypothesis Statement:

Suggested Recommendation/Replacement Behavior(s):

Positive Behavior Supports Attempted:

Behavior Intervention Plan

Student:	**DOB:**
School:	**Grade:**
Date:	**Case Manager:**

Goal for Plan:

Setting Events, Triggers, Contexts (Antecedents):

Hypothetical Function of Behaviors:

Behavior Intervention Plan

Noncompliance	**Prevention:** **Consequence:** **Follow-up:**
Argumentative Behaviors	**Prevention:** **Consequence:** **Follow-up:**
Social Skills	**Prevention:** **Consequence:** **Follow-up:**
Hyperactivity/ Impulsivity	**Prevention:** **Consequence:** **Follow-up:**

Interventions:	**Person(s) Responsible for Implementing Intervention:**

Review Date: ____________________

Signatures	**Role**
	Student
	Parent
	Administrator
	General Educator
	Special Educator
	Paraprofessional
	Mental Health Professional
	Other:
	Other:

CHAPTER 1

The Law and Students with Special Needs

Learning Outcomes

After reading this chapter, you should be able to:

- ❑ Explain the historical aspects of IDEA and how this impacts the IEP
- ❑ Define: Individuals with Disabilities Education Improvement Act (IDEA)
- ❑ Define: Free Appropriate Public Education (FAPE)
- ❑ Explain the law, at the Federal level, pertaining to students with special needs
- ❑ Discuss current trends in special education
- ❑ Discuss how biblical implications may impact decision-making concerning students with special needs
- ❑ Explain Neurodiversity
- ❑ Examine and explain how the current Education Secretary may impact special education

Vocabulary

- ❑ The Education of All Handicapped Children Act (EAHCA)
- ❑ Individuals with Individuals with Disabilities Education Act (IDEA)
- ❑ Free Appropriate Public Education (FAPE)
- ❑ Child with a disability
- ❑ Neurodiversity

The Law and Students with Special Needs

The historical aspects of special education law lay the foundation for supporting students with special needs. When it comes to the law and serving students with disabilities, it is important to have a basic understanding of how the law transpired, current lawful requirements, and how the law might change to better serve students as time progresses. Historical aspects of the law will allow you to understand and communicate the very foundation for why Individualized Education Plans (IEPs) exist and their initial intended purpose. Understanding the law as it currently exists is essential for meeting student needs, as well as for being intentional to ensure that students with disabilities and their families are not denied the rights afforded them by the law. Since all laws have the potential to change, as seen in the historical aspects of the laws regarding students with special needs, it is important to consider current trends and data to anticipate possible future changes. In this chapter, aspects of the law including historical, current, and potential elements, will be discussed. Additionally, biblical elements will be integrated to support you in planning, writing, and implementing an IEP from a Christian perspective.

Law Concerning Children with Disabilities: Historical Aspects

Prior to the enactment of laws to protect and serve children with disabilities, the outcomes for these individuals were grim at best. Many individuals were sent to live in state institutions designed for persons with mental disabilities or mental illness. Many of those institutions merely provided daily living essentials such as food, shelter, and clothing. Rarely were these persons with disabilities assessed and educated with the intent of helping them live a productive and fulfilling life as a contributing member of society. Many persons with disabilities were merely tolerated and shut away in those institutions. It was this mistreatment of individuals that inspired some people to take a second look at how persons with special needs were being treated by society.

One of the first rays of hope for persons with disabilities came to light in the 1950s and 1960s when the Federal government began to implement effective programs and services for early intervention and special education at the state level across the country. Some programs and services that paved the way to Federal laws for students with disabilities include:

1958: The Captioned Films Acts of 1958 (PL 85-905), which put captions on films for students who were deaf or hard of hearing

1959: The Training of Professional Personnel Act of 1959 (PL 86-158), which helped train leaders to educate children with mental disabilities

1961: The Teachers of the Deaf Act of 1961 (PL 87-276), which trained teachers for children who were deaf or hard of hearing

1965: The Elementary and Secondary Education Act (PL 89-10), which provided states with direct grant assistance to help educate children with disabilities

1965: The State Schools Act (PL 89-313) which also provided states with direct grant assistance to help educate children with disabilities

Though this is not an exhaustive list, these and other initiatives and programs paved the way for even more legislation to help students with disabilities and their families to achieve a higher standard of education and better quality of life.

In 1975, Public Law 94-142, **The Education of All Handicapped Children Act** (EAHCA, 1975), was enacted by congress to support states in protecting the rights of students with disabilities by meeting their needs and improving their educational outcomes. This legislation established supports for students with disabilities in the K-12 setting. The purposes of PL 94-142 were fourfold and included the following:

1. to ensure that all children with disabilities have available to them a free appropriate public education which emphasizes special education and related services designed to meet their unique needs
2. to ensure that the rights of children with disabilities and their parents are protected

3. to assist states and localities in providing for the education of all children with disabilities
4. to assess and ensure the effectiveness of efforts to educate all children with disabilities (EAHCA, 1975)

PL 94-142 was one of the first major Federal laws designed to make a positive difference for students with special needs and their families. This law was enacted to help ensure that students with special needs were no longer ostracized by society and sent away to institutions to merely exist. Certainly, it took years, even decades, to persuade a shift in the way society perceived and accepted this change, but the historical account of this shift is evidenced by the change in how students with special needs are served and supported in public schools today. This law was originally known as Public Law 94-142, the Education of All Handicapped Children Act; however, in 1990, amendments to the law were passed and the law was renamed the **Individuals with Disabilities Education Act** (IDEA).

The Individuals with Disabilities Education Act (IDEA)

Prior to IDEA, many students were denied access to educational opportunities. For example, in 1970 only one in five children with disabilities was educated in the U.S. school system. Additionally, laws excluding students who were deaf, blind, emotionally disturbed, or mentally handicapped were passed in many states (USDOE, 2007). These laws were meant to specifically exclude students based on their disability and deny those students educational opportunities. Isaiah 42:16 says,

> I will lead the blind by a way they do not know, in paths they do not know I will guide them, I will make darkness into light before them. And rugged places into plains. These are the things I will do, and I will not leave them undone. (New American Standard Bible)

The Lord specifically spoke of these students as well, but for a different purpose. His intention was to "lead" and "guide" the students. As we discuss the law, consider how different past laws would have been if they had been determined from a biblical perspective. Further, consider that if history could be rewritten and everyone treated students with disabilities the way the Lord intended by leading and guiding them, would it have ever been necessary for the government to pass protective laws? Though we are obviously not able to rewrite history, we do have the power to write our own history and contribute to the history of our students. Changing a society's perspective on students with special needs happens one person at a time.

I encourage you, as a future educator or parent, to compare past, present, and future treatment of students with special needs. In doing so, decide how you will contribute to society one decision at a time. When in an IEP meeting, how will you make decisions? Will you base your decision on the law, biblical implications, or both? My hope is that you will be determined to represent the Lord in every meeting and that when your students look back on their education, they will remember the godly teacher who led and guided them along the way. Though IDEA will be the guiding and foundational document that you will use, it should be your relationship with the Lord that ultimately drives your decision-making process. Some may say this suggests that we shirk the law and do what the Bible says. This is not the case. Remember that the Bible also says in Romans 13:1, "Let everyone be subject to the governing authorities, for there is no authority except that which God has established" (New International Version). The authorities that exist have been established by God. We are all subject to the law, but like the late Jerry Falwell senior said, "If it is Christian, it ought to be better." This means that the law should be our minimum requirement, and we should seek the Lord to see how we can make a child's life better based on the decisions that the Lord places on our hearts as we seek His guidance.

> *Though IDEA will be the guiding and foundational document that you will use, it should be your relationship with the Lord that ultimately drives decision-making process.*

PL 94-142, IDEA (1997, 2004) was enacted to ensure that all children with disabilities receive a free public education "to meet their unique needs and prepare them for further education, employment, and independent living" (American Psychiatric Association [APA], 2015). This was another victory for students with special needs and their families. As a result of PL 94-142, many students with disabilities began to see marked improvement in their educational outcomes. In the mid-1980s, there was an increase in the number of students with disabilities seeking employment opportunities and pursuing higher education. Students with disabilities, who historically had been considered uneducable, were now showing promise thanks to improvements in the law. Today, more students with special needs than ever are being served in the public-school system (Samuels, 2016).

Law Concerning Children with Disabilities: Current Aspects

Understanding current law regarding students with special needs will help to ensure that these students and their families are afforded their rights. Additionally, practicing lawful requirements will help meet the needs of students with disabilities by helping educators to be intentional in developing effective IEPs for these students. This is why IDEA exists.

To understand the law, it is important to understand the term "child with a disability." According to both the 2004 and present-day IDEA, the definition for a **child with a disability** is as follows:

(A) In general

The term child with a disability means a child:

i. with intellectual disabilities, hearing impairments (including deafness), speech or language impairments, visual impairments (including blindness), serious emotional disturbance (referred to in this chapter as "emotional disturbance"), orthopedic impairments, autism, traumatic brain injury, other health impairments, or specific learning disabilities; and
ii. who, by reason thereof, needs special education and related services.

(B) Child aged 3 through 9

The term child with a disability for a child aged 3 through 9 (or any subset of that age range, including ages 3 through 5), may, at the discretion of the state and the local educational agency, include a child:

i. experiencing developmental delays, as defined by the state and as measured by appropriate diagnostic instruments and procedures, in 1 or more of the following areas: physical development; cognitive development; communication development; social or emotional development; or adaptive development; and
ii. who, by reason thereof, needs special education and related services (20 U.S.C. § 1401[3][A][B]).

IDEA is a law that includes six main principles to guarantee that all children with disabilities, as defined above, are provided a **free appropriate public education** (FAPE) that meets their individual needs. FAPE is defined as:

> Recipients operating federally funded programs must provide education and related services free of charge to students with disabilities and their parents or guardians. Provision of a free education is the provision of education and related services without cost to the person with a disability or his or her parents or guardians, except for fees equally imposed on nondisabled persons or their parents or guardians. (U.S. Department of Education [USDOE], Office of Civil Rights, 2010, n.p.)

IDEA has been amended multiple times; the latest amendment was in 2004, and it includes the following six guiding principles:

1. All children between the ages of 6 and 17 with disabilities must be served by the local public-school district; if education is provided to ages before or after these ages, then the state must provide education services to children with disabilities within those age ranges.

2. Testing and evaluation must be free from discrimination or bias based on race, culture, language, or disability. The testing must be comprehensive and determine whether special education is appropriate for the child.
3. The education is provided at no cost to the family and provided at public expense. An IEP is to be set forth explaining the nature of the disability.
4. This education is also to be provided in the least restrictive environment possible, meaning that students with disabilities should participate to the greatest extent with nondisabled peers in academic, elective, and other activities during the school day.
5. Safeguards must be put into effect to protect the child and their family's rights during the evaluation process. Consent must be obtained by the legal guardian prior to beginning the evaluation and for all decisions impacting the educational needs of the child. Parents have the right to disagree with the school's evaluation and have an independent evaluation completed.
6. Parents and students with disabilities are to be part of the evaluation process and implementation of special education services (Woodworth, 2016, pp. 54–55).

If we break these down into simpler terms, the list would look something like this:

1. Free Appropriate Public Education
2. Appropriate Evaluation
3. IEP
4. Least Restrictive Environment
5. Parent Participation
6. Procedural Protections

© Rena Schild/Shutterstock.com

Throughout this book, we will examine each of these principles; however, it is important to note that IDEA is a Federal law that mandates the special education process. This book has been structured in accordance with the Federal law, but it is critical that you understand that states may also choose to add state-level policies and procedures above and beyond what the Federal law requires, and those may impact the decisions you make regarding the IEP process. It is always important to consult your own state, district, and school to fully understand the policies, procedures, and regulations that are required for your specific situation. Additionally, it is imperative that federal law and state mandates align with students' and teachers' needs. As we discuss the law, consider what your part may be in either influencing the law, or supporting it as written, to best meet the needs of your students.

Since the passage of PL 94-142 and IDEA, students with disabilities have received supports and services and have begun to demonstrate increased academic ability, which have paved the way for inclusion in post-high school career opportunities and post-secondary education (Hart, Grigal, & Weir, 2010). According to the U.S. Department of Education (2007), accomplishments for students with disabilities that are a direct result of IDEA include:

- Educating more students in local schools rather than in separate schools or institutions
- Improved high school graduation rates
- Increased post-secondary enrollment
- Improved post-high school employment rates

IDEA guarantees a free and appropriate education in the K-12 setting in the least restrictive environment, and schools are legally accountable for identifying student's needs, determining modification and accommodations, and implementing a plan via each student's IEP.

Research

In a recent study conducted by Zirkel and Hetrick (2017), research revealed important information for educators and families to make note of. Their study focused on the frequency and outcomes of alleged IDEA procedural violations in four categories as follows:

1. IEP components
2. IEP team
3. Parent participation
4. IEP development

Results of the study revealed that parent participation procedural violations were the most frequently adjudicated. The outcome of these court cases ruled in favor of the school districts at a ratio of approximately 3 to 1 (Zirkel & Hetrick, 2017). Why is this important to understand? This information reveals two important elements for educators and parents. The first is that many parents interpret the actions of educators as a violation of their procedural rights. The second is that courts tend to rule in favor of the school district for this category, which suggests that there is a strong perception divide between the parents and the school districts when it comes to parental rights. We will look at this more closely in the chapter on parents, but for now, let us consider how this situation might be avoided. In his book, *Walking with God in the Classroom: Christian Approaches to Teaching and Learning*, Van Brummelen (2009) states that classrooms cannot function effectively unless harmonious relationships exist. The same principle holds true for relationships established while planning, writing, and implementing IEPs. One way to escape a negative IEP experience and avoid landing in court is to establish a harmonious relationship with all persons participating in the IEP experience; this includes parents, students, general education teachers, special education teachers, administrators, counselors, therapists, and other support service and specialized service personnel. In the Bible, Philippians 2:3 says, "do nothing through rivalry or through conceit, but in humility, each counting others better than himself" (World English Bible). Evoking this biblical directive, while intentionally building positive relationships throughout the IEP process, may just be the key to truly focusing on how we can best serve and improve the outcomes for the students entrusted to us by the Lord.

Free Appropriate Public Education

The foundational law for students with special needs is IDEA. One of the fundamental principles supporting the law is FAPE. In 1982, in a landmark decision in the *Board of Education v. Rowley*, the Supreme Court delivered two essential elements for determining whether or not a district met its FAPE obligations. These two elements are procedural and substantive. Specifically, the Rowley court case made a decision based on two questions:

1. Did the school district comply with the various applicable procedures? and
2. Is the IEP "reasonably calculated to enable the child to receive educational benefits?" (pp. 206–207).

The 2004 amendments to the IDEA changed this a bit more to state that:

1. Procedural violations must have impeded the child's right to FAPE,
2. Caused a denial of educational benefits, or
3. Significantly hindered the parent's opportunity to participate in the IEP decision-making process (20 U.S.C. § 1415[f][3][E]).

© Rena Schild/Shutterstock.com

All of these elements must be considered when planning, writing, and implementing an IEP, and we will discuss them throughout the book as we learn more about the IEP process. In order to uphold the law, one must understand the law. The same holds true for the Bible. When I was a young mother, a wise man told me that I can only teach my child the parts of the Bible that I know. That was extremely convicting and challenging. I wanted my children to be raised in a godly home and I wanted them to know and love the Lord, but I could only teach them what I knew. This catapulted me into spending more time in prayer with the Lord and into learning more about Scripture. As we progress through this book, the law and Scripture will be interwoven in order to help you understand what the law says and how these lawful requirements can be achieved through a biblical worldview.

Law Concerning Children with Disabilities: Potential Aspects

Since we are unable to predict the future, this section is mostly speculative. However, we are able to use past information to help predict future trends and even to guide and direct those trends. As I began planning this book, I felt a slight sting every time I wrote the words "student with a disability" or "student with special needs." Even though this is considered proper "person-first" language, it still had a negative connotation to it. It was as if the Lord were saying "I made them exactly the way I intended." Psalm 139:13–16 in the Bible says:

> For you created my inmost being; you knit me together in my mother's womb. I praise you because I am fearfully and wonderfully made; your works are wonderful; I know that full well. My frame was not hidden from you when I was made in the secret place. When I was woven together in the depths of the earth, your eyes saw my unformed body. All the days ordained for me were written in your book before one of them came to be.

The thought occurred to me that it would be great if, as a society, we could focus on the ability rather than the disability. However, many people have already thought of this and have taken action to persuade society's thoughts concerning students with special needs through the term neurodiversity.

Neurodiversity

One current trend in special education is a term called "neurodiversity." Though this term was coined in the early 1990s, it seems to be gaining momentum. **Neurodiversity** can be defined as an "understanding that neurological differences are to be honored and respected just like any other human variation, including diversity in race, ethnicity, gender identity, religion, sexual orientation, and so on" (Armstrong, 2017, p. 10). Some of the major differences in current special education practices and those grounded in neurodiversity are noted in the following chart:

	Current Special Education Practice	**Neurodiversity Practice**
Main Focus	Disability	Diversity
Assessment	To detect disability or deficits	Assesses strengths and challenges
Instructional Approach	Remediating weaknesses	Building on strengths to overcome challenges
Theoretical Foundations	Genetics, neurobiology	Evolutionary psychobiology, social and ecological

Adapted from Armstrong (2017), *A Tale of Two Special Education Paradigms.*

The table above represents a portion of the differences noted by Armstrong (2017). Though we will not all agree that this information is factual, there is some validity in some of what is proposed. For example, if would be hard to argue that when testing students today, the main focus is to determine a student's deficit. Once determined, then doctors and educators come up with a plan to support the student in that deficit. For instance, a student who is struggling to read may be tested to determine the cause of the deficit. It may be determined that this student has dyslexia. Since the student has dyslexia, the teacher is then able to write an IEP to support the students reading deficit. What would this same scenario look like if it was approached from a neurodiversity perspective? Perhaps this same student would be tested to determine strengths and weaknesses. This may reveal that the student has dyslexia, but it can also reveal that the student has strong analytical skills and is a strong auditory learner. At that point, a plan could be devised to use the student's strength to help him overcome the reading deficit. The focus shifts slightly to the strength rather than the weakness. The weakness is not ignored, but the perspective is intentionally shifted to the strength. Tests similar to this concept are being conducted today, and it is hopeful that we will continue to see an increase in their use to determine both the strengths and deficits of students with special needs.

Another example to consider is the theoretical foundations of neurodiversity. This difference would be considered controversial by many Christians, as many Christians do not believe in evolution as is stated on the table. The intention of this section is not to debate whether evolution is fact or fiction; the intention of this chapter is to bring awareness to the reader that there are current trends in special education. As a Christian, we can help influence what those trends are. If you see a trend that you do not agree with, what will you do about it? How will you react? Is it possible to take the elements of trends that align with scripture and implement those while ignoring ones that conflict with scripture? These are all questions that will ultimately need to be answered by you as you plan, write, and implement an IEP.

Federal and State Support for Special Education

Another trend to carefully consider is the potential transformation of education caused when there is a change in government officials. With the 2016 election of President Donald Trump, many people wisely anticipated changes in education. The first major change for education in general was with the appointment of Betsy DeVos as Education Secretary.

Shortly after her appointment, DeVos stated that she believes that special education decisions should be made at the state-level. This is important for educators and families to be aware of, as this may influence both parties to make major decisions. For example, the *Houston Chronicle* reported that the Texas Education Agency

© a katz/Shutterstock.com

Betsy DeVos, Donald Trump, Mike Pence.

put a limit on the number of students who would receive special education services in 2004. The number, which appears to have been randomly chosen, was 8.5% of students. This random limit prohibited tens of thousands of students from receiving needed services (Rosenthal, 2016b). Since there is a limited number of students who will be served via special education services, this may cause many families who are denied services or believe their child is under-serviced, to move their family to a different location. Ultimately, this places the financial burden on neighboring states that are known to be more generous when it comes to students with special needs. Over time, this may cause neighboring states to become financially overwhelmed with students with special needs and may cause them to implement stricter laws and limitations such as those practiced in Texas. This has the potential to have a negative impact of students with special needs unless this is regulated at the Federal level. As stated above, the limit in Texas is reported as fact in the Houston *Chronicle* (Rosenthal, 2016a), but the remaining scenario is speculative based on limited information. However, one can see the rationale behind how this could potentially transpire.

In 2021, Joe Biden took office as President of the United States. He chose Miguel Cardona as Education Secretary. According to President Biden, "Dr. Cardona has a proven track record as an innovative leader who will fight for all students, and for a better, fairer, more successful education system, he will also strive to eliminate long-standing inequities and close racial and socioeconomic opportunity gaps—and expand access to community colleges, training, and public four-year colleges and universities to improve student success and grow a stronger, more prosperous, and more inclusive middle class" (Murakami, 2021, n.p.). Cardona, testifying at his confirmation hearing, told lawmakers, "The passion I have for public education stems from my belief that it is the best lever for economic success and prosperity in Connecticut and the belief that public education is still the great equalizer. It was for me." Time will tell what impact the new Education Secretary will have on education in general and specifically on special education.

Conclusion

Though an IEP is typically written in a small classroom, the impact of the law is experienced nation-wide. As you begin to learn more about the IEP process, keep in mind that this is not just a matter of getting a student through a school year until the student leaves your classroom and becomes someone else's student. The decisions you make will impact this child's entire life, and possibly even eternity. In order to keep history from repeating itself, it is important that we recognize why these laws were necessary in the first place. Additionally, educators absolutely must know the law. The only way to ensure that the law is followed and students and parents are allocated their rights, is for educators to know what those rights are. Additionally, keeping up with current trends and major occurrences at the Federal level will help educators decide how they will help influence a society when it comes to serving students with special needs.

Chapter Highlights

Historical aspects of the law will allow you to understand and communicate the very foundation for why IEPs exist and their initial intended purpose.

Understanding the law as it currently exists is essential for meeting student needs, as well as for being intentional to ensure that students with disabilities and their families are not denied the rights afforded them by the law.

In the 1950s and 1960s when the Federal government began to implement effective programs and services for early intervention and special education at the state level across the country.

In 1975, Public Law 94-142, **The Education of All Handicapped Children Act** (EAHCA, 1975), was enacted by congress to support states in protecting the rights of students with disabilities by meeting their needs and improving their educational outcomes in a K-12 setting.

PL 94-142 was one of the first major Federal laws designed to make a positive difference for students with special needs and their families.

This means that the law should be our minimum requirement, and we should seek the Lord to see how we can make a child's life better based on the decisions that the Lord places on our hearts as we seek His guidance.

IDEA is a law that includes six main principles to guarantee that all children with disabilities are provided a **free appropriate public education** (FAPE) that meets their individual needs.

It is critical that you understand that states may also choose to add state-level policies and procedures above and beyond what the Federal law requires, and those may impact the decisions you make regarding the IEP process.

It is always important to consult your own state, district, and school to fully understand the policies, procedures, and regulations that are required for your specific situation.

It is imperative that federal law and state mandates align with students' and teachers' needs.

Since the passage of PL 94-142 and IDEA, students with disabilities have received supports and services and have begun to demonstrate increased academic ability, which have paved the way for inclusion in post-high school career opportunities and postsecondary education (Hart et al., 2010).

One way to avoid court is to establish a harmonious relationship with all persons participating in the IEP experience including parents, students, general education teachers, special education teachers, administrators, counselors, therapists, and other support service and specialized service personnel.

Neurodiversity can be defined as an "understanding that neurological differences are to be honored and respected just like any other human variation, including diversity in race, ethnicity, gender identity, religion, sexual orientation, and so on" (Armstrong, 2017, p. 10).

In 2021, Joe Biden took office as President of the United States. He chose Miguel Cardona as Education Secretary.

Chapter Review Questions

1. Explain how the historical treatment of students with special needs impacted the current laws governing these students.
2. How will the Bible impact the decisions you make for a student with special needs?
3. Name several Scriptures, other than those mentioned in the chapter, that will influence your decision-making for students with special needs.
4. Define a "child with a disability" according to the law.
5. Name the six guiding elements of the current IDEA law in simple terms.
6. Name four accomplishments for students with special needs that are a direct result of IDEA.
7. What foundational information will you use to make decisions regarding each student for whom you are conducting or participating in an IEP for? Explain this from a lawful and biblical perspective.
8. What are the guiding questions regarding FAPE? How will this impact your decision-making process?
9. Explain neurodiversity.
10. As the new Education Secretary, what impact might Betsy DeVos have on special education? Conduct more research on her stance on special education and expound on how this might impact teachers in a special education classroom.

Additional Resources

- To read the entire IDEA law visit this website: http://uscode.house.gov/view.xhtml?path=/prelim@title20/chapter33&edition=prelim
- For guidance concerning IDEA, visit this website: https://sites.ed.gov/idea/
- To read the story reported in the *Houston Chronicle*, visit this website: http://www.houstonchronicle.com/denied/1/

References

American Psychiatric Association (APA). (2015). *Individuals with Disabilities Education Act*. Retrieved from http://www.apa.org/about/gr/issues/disability/idea.aspx

Armstrong, T. (2017). Neurodiversity: The future of special education? *Educational Leadership*, *74*(7), 10–16.

Board of Education v. Rowley, 458 U.S. 176 (1982) (pp. 206–207).

Hart, D., Grigal, M., & Weir, C. (2010). Expanding the paradigm: Postsecondary education options for individuals with autism spectrum disorder and intellectual disabilities. *Focus on Autism and Other Developmental Disabilities*, *25*(3), 134–150. doi:10.1177/1088357610373759

Individuals with Disabilities Education Improvement Act of 2004. (2004). Retrieved from: http://idea.ed.gov/

Murakami, K. (2021, January 4). Biden's choice for education secretary. *Inside Higher Ed*. https://www.insidehighered.com/news/2021/01/04/biden-selects-miguel-cardona-education-secretary

Rosenthal, B. M. (2016a, September 1). Denied: How Texas keeps tens of thousands of kids out of special education. *The Houston Chronicle*. Retrieved from: http://www.chron.com/local/article/Denied-How-Texas-keeps-tens-of-thousands-of-kids-9215602.php

Rosenthal, B. M. (2016b). Denied: How Texas keeps tens of thousands of kids out of special education. *The Houston Chronicle*. Retrieved from: http://www.chron.com/local/article/Denied-How-Texas-keeps-tens-of-thousands-of-kids-9215602.php

Samuels, C. A. (2016). Number of U.S. students in special education ticks upward. *Education Week*, *35*(28), 1, 12.

The Education of All Handicapped Children Act (EAHCA, 1975).

U.S. Department of Education (USDOE), Office of Civil Rights (2010). *Free appropriate public education for students with disabilities: Requirements under section 504 of the Rehabilitation Act of 1973*. Retrieved from: https://www2.ed.gov/about/offices/list/ocr/docs/edlite-FAPE504.html

Van Brummelen, H. (2009). *Walking with God in the classroom: Christian approaches to teaching and learning* (3rd ed.). Colorado Springs, CO: Purposeful Design Publications.

Woodworth, J. (2016). IEPs, 504 plans and behavior contracts. *The Exceptional Parent*, *46*(9), 54–56.

Zirkel, P. A., & Hetrick, A. (2017). Which procedural parts of the IEP process are the most judicially vulnerable? *Exceptional Children*, *83*(2), 219–235. doi:10:1177/0014402916651849

CHAPTER 2

Parents and the Individualized Education Plan Process

Learning Outcomes

After reading this chapter, you should be able to:

- ❑ Define a parent as determined by IDEA
- ❑ Explain the educator's responsibility when a student has anything other than two married, biological parents
- ❑ Discuss Romans 12:3–4 in terms of the educator's leadership role in the IEP process
- ❑ Describe the rights of parents of a child with a disability according to IDEA
- ❑ Explain the significance of relationships in the IEP process
- ❑ Describe the important elements of FAPE
- ❑ Discuss how to help a parent set up a learning environment at home
- ❑ Name and describe benefits and barriers to parental participation in the IEP process

Vocabulary

- ❑ Parent
- ❑ Culturally Responsive Practices

Parents and the Individualized Education Plan Process

In 1975, parents were given the role of team members and decision-makers regarding the education of their child in the Education of All Handicapped Children Act, which is known today as Individuals with Disabilities Education Act (IDEA). Though parents practiced this right for 22 years, Congress believed that the parents' role needed to be further established and clarified. In 1997, IDEA mandated that schools provide an opportunity for active participation of parents as decision-makers for their child. Before proceeding through this chapter on parents, it is important to understand the definition of a parent according to the law.

Definition of a Parent

According to IDEA (2004), the definition of a **parent** is as follows:

(23) Parent

The term parent means:

A. a natural, adoptive, or foster parent of a child (unless a foster parent is prohibited by State law from serving as a parent);
B. a guardian (but not the State if the child is a ward of the State);
C. an individual acting in the place of a natural or adoptive parent (including a grandparent, step-parent, or other relative) with whom the child lives, or an individual who is legally responsible for the child's welfare; or
D. except as used in sections 1415(b)(2) and 1439(a)(5) of this title, an individual assigned under either of those sections to be a surrogate parent. (20 U.S.C. § 1401[23], [A][B][C][D])

Now that the term parent has been defined, let's discuss the parental role a bit further. Since parents play an instrumental role in developing an Individualized Education Plan (IEP), and are required team members, reaching out to them and making them feel wanted and included is an essential element of the Christian educator's role. As you begin and proceed through the IEP process, note and remember that Romans 12:3b-4 says,

> Do not think of yourself more highly then you ought, but rather think of yourself with sober judgment, in accordance with the faith God has distributed to each of you. For just as each of us has one body with many members, these members do not all have the same function.

If we think of the IEP team as one body with multiple functions, we may more fully understand the importance of each member. The parent can contribute valuable information that may truly be in the best interest of the child. Just as the parent is not able to contribute the expertise you have as an educator; you are not able to contribute valuable information that the parent has as the parent. Both voices are needed in order to allow the team to fully function at its greatest capacity, and this is reflected in the words of Proverbs 31:8: Speak out on behalf of the voiceless, and for the rights of all who are vulnerable (Common English Bible). If one voice is missing, then a critical component of the team is missing; and thus, the child's education is likely to suffer. In most cases, parents will be an integral part of the IEP process, which makes it imperative that educators understand the rights that parents have. This includes limitations placed on them by the law such as in the case of divorce.

If we think of the IEP team as one body with multiple functions, we may more fully understand the importance of each member.

Divorce

The divorce rate in the United States is 50% and climbing (American Psychological Association [APA], 2017). Additionally, having a child with a disability may increase the risk for divorce, depending on the specific disability of the child and depending on the different seasons of life being experienced. For example, divorce rates typically increase during a child's adolescent years (Namkung, Song, Greenberg, Mailick, & Floyd, 2015). Since IDEA has defined a parent, it is important to elaborate on divorced parents and your responsibility as an educator.

In cases of divorce, the courts determine which parent has legal authority to make educational decisions. Custody documents typically state which parent(s) have the legal right to make decisions regarding the child's education, and to what extent those decisions can be made if both parents do have a voice in those decisions.

> Schools should never assume that a parent gives truthful information regarding who does and does not have decision-making rights, and therefore legal documentation should be obtained if the child has anything other than two biological, married parents as the decision makers. (Losinski, Katsivannis, White, & Wiseman, 2015, p. 144)

According to IDEA, if a court order designates a specific person as the educational decision-maker, that person has the rights of the parent (34 C.F.R. § 300.30[b][2]). Thus, it is essential for the IEP team to be aware of the marital status of the parents and, in the case of divorce, obtain copies of documents from the parents that describe the person(s) designated as the decision-maker for the child.

Since a multitude of personalities and preferences are represented in a school, it is important for all parties involved to remain focused on what is best for the student, despite these differences. Every person on the committee adds value, but oftentimes the value of the parent is underrated. Though educators have been trained how to teach and should certainly bring a wealth of knowledge and training to the meeting, parents typically have a perspective of their child that teachers are not often privy to. Some of the most successful IEP meetings are the ones where the team leader is able to draw on every participant's strengths and mesh that information into one cohesive, beneficial document aimed at helping the student meet his or her fullest potential. In this chapter, we will focus on learning about the law regarding parents' rights and the benefits and barriers to parent participation in the IEP process.

Given that parental participation is such a critical feature of IDEA, it is essential that IEP team members understand the family dynamics and the legal implications for parental participation. This chapter offers only a glimpse of detail, as it is meant to stress the importance of including parents in the IEP process and the legal reasons for doing so. It is also meant to communicate some of the basic rights of the parents. In order to fully understand the dynamics of parents and the law, please see the actual law as well as the additional resources listed at the end of the chapter.

The Law Regarding Parental Rights

Many parents and educators are intimidated by the laws governing IEPs. Some elements of the law are easier to interpret and administer than others. Since we have just read the chapter on the law, it may be easier for you to understand the law than it would be for a parent who has never read about it. Educators and parents need to understand the legal rights governing the IEP process regarding parents in order to make decisions that abide by the law and are in the best interest of the child. According to IDEA, parents of a child with a disability have the right:

> To examine all records relating to such child and to participate in meetings with respect to the identification, evaluation, and educational placement of the child, and the provision of a free appropriate

> public education to such child, and to obtain independent educational evaluation of the child. (20.U.S.C. §1415[b][1])

To make this a bit easier to understand, let's break it down further.

Examine All Records

According to the law, parents may "examine all records relating to" their child. This means that parents have the right to review all the documentation made about their child. All school personnel would be wise to choose their words wisely when documenting information about a child. Stating factual and accurate information from various situations while avoiding negative and derogatory comments is essential. It is also important to document often. An IEP meeting should have multiple documents that have been created over time. This information should reveal a starting point (such as the present level of academic and functional achievement) and progress made from that starting point to specific goals. Details are important to note along the way, as it is easy to forget everything that the student has accomplished or needs to work on while participating in an IEP meeting. If the information has been documented, the meeting will contain more accurate and robust information.

Participate in Meetings

Additionally, parents have the right to participate in meetings that relate to:

- Identification
- Evaluation
- Placement

This means that parents have the right to attend more than just a single IEP meeting; they have the right to be active participants in the educational process of their child. Not all parents will want to be involved to the same degree, and not all parents will be able to be fully engaged in the process. As a teacher, it is your responsibility to encourage parental participation and to invite them to attend the meetings, but it is not your responsibility to ensure that they attend; some will and some will not. This part of the law requires that the parent be invited to participate.

Parents must be formally given written notice prior to an IEP meeting. This notice must include the purpose of the meeting, the time, the date, and names of the participants including the participants' position, as shown in the example meeting notice below.

Liberty Academic School

Liberty Academic School
XXXX XXXX XXXXXX
XXXXXXX XXXXXX
XXXXXXX XXXXXX
Telephone: XXXXXX
Fax: XXXXXXXXXX
Email: xxxxx@xxxx.com
Website: www.xxxxxxx.com

Individualized Education Plan
Meeting Notice

Name: David and Mary Smith Date: September 7, 2022

You are invited to attend an IEP meeting for your child: Brett Smith

Meeting Details:

Date: 9/20/22

Time: 1:30

Location: D221

Purpose of Meeting:

______ IEP Development
___✓___ IEP Review
___✓___ Discuss Services[1]
___✓___ Transition[2]
______ Manifestation Determination
______ Other

[1]If the purpose of this meeting is to discuss services, service personnel may be invited.

[2]If the purpose of the meeting is to discuss transition, the student will be invited.

If you are unable to attend the meeting at this scheduled time and location, or if you would like additional information prior to the meeting, please contact the IEP team leader below to reschedule.

Kelly Garman	Kgarman@email.com	(111)-111-1111
Team Leader	Email	Phone Number

Participants Involved:
Below is a list of participants invited to this IEP meeting. Attendance is required.

Name of Participant	Position
David & Mary Smith	Father and Mother
Brett Smith	Student
Shonda Miller	Administrator
Kelly Garman	Special Education Teacher, Team Leader
Stuart Fisher	General Education Teacher
Dr. Nathaniel Salinas	Guidance Counselor
Russ Greer	Speech/Language Therapist

Individualized Education Plan
Meeting Notice, continued

Please keep the first page, and return this page to the team leader.

Kelly Garman	Kgarman@email.com	(111)-111-1111
Team Leader	Email	Phone Number

Meeting Details:

Date: 9/20/22

Time: 1:30

Location: D221

Based on the date and location above:

__✓__ I WILL attend the IEP meeting as scheduled

_____ I WILL NOT attend the IEP meeting as scheduled

If you will not attend the meeting. Please complete the following:

_____ Please contact me to reschedule the meeting.

_____ I can participate via WebEx or ________________

_____ Please hold the meeting without me.

_____ I give permission to proceed without a meeting.

_____ If no response, proceed with meeting.

_____ I would like to share my input via other means (email, telephone, mail).

David Smith	9/10/22
Signature of Parent	Date

By listing the attendees, you may help communicate the significance of the meeting and encourage the parents to become active participants in the process. This table may also be intimidating to some parents; thus, it is important to work toward building the relationship with the parents to encourage their involvement even when they may feel intimidated. Since relationships drive decision-making, this is one of the most critical elements of the IEP process, but it is one that is often overlooked and undervalued. Establishing relationships can have positive or detrimental results.

This response from the parents' provides documentation that the parents received the IEP notification, as well as their intensions for attendance. The IEP Meeting Response document should become part of the student's permanent IEP file.

Free Appropriate Public Education

IDEA was enacted to ensure students receive a Free Appropriate Public Education (FAPE) regardless of their ability. Many parents of a student with special needs have come to expect much more for their student from the school system than was provided in the past.

> IDEA strives not only to grant equal access to students with disabilities, but also to provide additional special education services and procedural safeguards to those individuals. Special education services are designed to be individualized to meet the unique needs of students with disabilities and are to be offered in the least restrictive environment. Such services are provided in accordance with an IEP specifically tailored to the unique needs of each student. (Rusu & Weisman, 2015, p. 255)

As an educator, many of these decisions will be your responsibility, especially if you are the team leader. The word "appropriate" in this part of the law, is somewhat subjective, and appropriateness should always be determined based on the specific unique needs of the individual student. Parental input should be solicited in terms of the law in order to ensure that parental rights for a FAPE are not violated. If a team member will not attend the IEP meeting, the school needs to have written permission from the parent excusing the member from the meeting. All members may not be necessary in all meetings, but it is a best-practice to ensure that parents are aware of who the attendees are well in advance of the meeting. Below is an example of a Team Member Excusal Request form.

Liberty Academic School
XXXX XXXX XXXXXX
XXXXXXX XXXXXX
XXXXXXX XXXXXX
Telephone: XXXXXX
Fax: XXXXXXXXXX
Email: xxxxx@xxxx.com
Website: www.xxxxxxx.com

Individualized Education Plan
Team Member Excusal Request

If the team member's area of curriculum, related services, or expertise will be discussed, the team member may be excused, but must provide written comments and submit for approval 10 days prior to the meeting. If the team members' area of curriculum, related services, or expertise will not be discussed, the team member may be excused without written documentation.

The following team members have requested to be excused from the meeting.

Name of Participant	Position	Reason
Russ Greer	Speech/Language Therapist	Mr. Greer is having surgery on this date and requests to be updated with Brett's needs and will accommodate his speech schedule as needed.

The excusal request is for the following date:

Student Name: Brett Smith

IEP Meeting Date: September 20, 2022

Meeting Location: D221

✓ **I agree to excuse the above team member from the meeting.**

David Smith
Signature of Parent

9/10/22
Date

Shonda Miller
Signature of Administrator/District Representative

September 10, 2022
Date

Independent Educational Evaluation

Parents also have the legal right to request an independent evaluation of their child. What does this mean for you as an educator? This means that, like a teacher or administrator, a parent has the right to request that a student be formally evaluated or tested for special education services. If the parent is requesting the evaluation, the parent must give a written recommendation to the school administration. If the teacher or administrator requests the evaluation, the parent must be notified of the request and the parent must provide consent prior to the administration of the evaluation of the student.

School counselors and psychologists are not able to diagnose mental health or medical conditions and may refer the student to a primary care physician or another specialist. The evaluation may consist of multiple tests to assess cognitive, behavioral, developmental, and physical capacities. These tests are then scored and reviewed to determine if the child has a disability that requires special education services (Woodworth, 2016).

Benefits of Parent Participation

Encouraging Parent Participation

According to Henderson and Berla (1994),

The most accurate predictor of a student's achievement in school is not income or social status but the extent to which that student's family is able to:

1. Create a home environment that encourages learning
2. Express high (but not unrealistic) expectations for their children's achievement and future careers
3. Become involved in their children's education at school and in the community (p. 160)

The more we can support parents in this endeavor, the more likely it is that we can help their child succeed. There are many benefits of having parents involved in the IEP process, but the most significant benefits are directly related to student outcomes. How can educators encourage parents to be a positive part of the IEP process that will benefit the student the most? One way is to help them create an environment that encourages learning.

Parental Participation Encourages Learning

As an educator, you can teach parents to be teachers at home. This may seem strange, but many parents are dependent on you to teach their child because they may either feel ill-equipped or they are ill-equipped, but with some guidance from the teacher, most parents can become a teacher at home. So, how can we teach parents how to create a learning environment at home? This will look different for different families, but for the most part, we want to teach parents to express a love for learning and reading.

© Arieliona/Shutterstock.com

Create a Work Space

Just as a student typically has a specific seat at school to complete his assignments, it is just as important for productivity for a student to have a place at home to complete homework. This is especially true since many students had to change how they learned due to COVID-19. Following COVID-19, schools may have chosen to continue teaching virtually, transitioned to a hybrid model, or they may have fully resumed face-to-face learning in a school building. Regardless of the learning model, students need a workspace to learn. For some students, it may be at the kitchen table, but ideally, it will be at a small desk or table away from the busyness of the kitchen. When creating a workspace, it is important to keep the individual needs of the student in mind. Some students learn better with music or the TV on in the background, while others need to be in a perfectly quiet environment. Due to limited space in the home, some students may need to find a creative workspace such as on a porch, on the stairs, in the basement, or any number of other creative spaces. One family allowed their child to work underneath the kitchen table, which had a table cloth over it, and on a blanket and pillows, because this allowed the student to work and not be in the way while mom cooked dinner, but it also made the student feel like he had his very own space. Being creative and flexible may allow for unusual solutions.

Create a Routine

The student's parents can be taught to have a routine that works best for their family situation. Many people think of coming directly home from school, having a snack, and getting right to work on homework. This will work well for many families, but it will not work well for all families. This may especially be true for students with special needs who may need a longer break or may work better just before bedtime. When creating a routine, it is important that the parents choose a routine that will work for their family. If a routine is chosen that does not fit the family's needs, the routine will fail. Be flexible and allow for change when change is needed. As students grow and mature, their needs will change; thus, routines should change accordingly.

Accountability

Teach the parents to hold the student accountable and to follow through with their work. Most people work harder and smarter when they are accountable to someone. Though the student is accountable to the teacher, a student who is also accountable to a parent for homework will produce homework that is more accurate and will do so in a timelier fashion. As a teacher, you can encourage the parents to hold their child accountable by communicating the expectations for the student in an organized and consistent manner. When the educator communicates student expectations on a daily or weekly basis, the parent will then be able to use that information to assist the student to live up to those expectations. This is a win-win situation.

Parental Participation Encourages High Achievement Expectations

Expressing an expectation of high achievement communicates a belief in the student's ability. It is always appropriate to express high expectations for a student, but these expectations must also always be achievable so that the student is not set up for failure. When it comes to setting goals for the student's IEP, the goals need to be realistically achievable.

When we have high expectations for our students, they tend to live up to that expectation. The opposite is also true. How many times have you heard a parent say, "I'm not surprised that my child is failing math, I couldn't do math when I was his age either?" Statements like this excuse a student from learning and should be discouraged. Many parents never think of it that way unless it is pointed out. It is best for educators to point this out before a statement like this is said. This could be done in the form of a "Parent Newsletter," that way parents get the information without being targeted or called out.

Become Involved in the School and Community

Parents should be encouraged to attend school events and events in the community. Parents who are more involved in the school tend to have students who achieve more because they are familiar with what is going on in the school.

When parents are involved, the IEP team will have the opportunity to become more aware of the child's home environment, as parental involvement allows for more open communication. This goes back to developing a relationship with the family. When a trusting relationship has been established, parents and educators tend to be more open and honest about the reality of the situation both at home and at school. This increases the IEP teams' understanding of the child's home life and increases the parents' awareness of the child's life at school.

Parental Participation Encourages Commitment

When a trusting relationship is established which shows that teachers are committed to the student, parents may gain an understanding that the teacher desires what is best for the child and does not just see the IEP process as a part of their job requirement (Blue-Banning, Summers, Franklin, Nelson, & Beegle, 2004). Parents may perceive educators as reluctant to collaborate if they do not intentionally ask about and actively listen to their perspectives and goals for their children (Turnbull, Turnbull, Erwin, Soodak, & Shogren, 2011). Because committed relationships require more than just a once-a-year meeting, it is important to be intentional about engaging in positive interactions throughout the school year.

To convey commitment to families, educators should demonstrate through their words and actions that their focus is on the best interests of the child (Haines, Gross, Bule-Banning, Francis, & Turnbull, 2015). This can be done by regularly communicating the child's progress and other positive experiences to families, rather than only problems (Rodriguez, Blatz, & Elbaum, 2014). That way, the parents receive information that builds a relationship instead of only hearing from the educator when the student has not lived up to expectations.

Barriers to Parent Participation

To stress the importance of parental participation in the IEP process and the education of the student with special needs, Congress emphasized the need "for strengthening the role and responsibility of parents and ensuring that families of such children have meaningful opportunities to participate in the education of their children at school and at home" (20 U.S.C. § 1400[c][5][B]). As an educator, you can help to remove or minimize many of the barriers that may prevent parental participation such as communication, cultural barriers, and logistical barriers.

Communication

Though communication may be a benefit to the IEP process, it may also be a barrier. Communication may be the predominant reason parents may not be as involved in the IEP process as possible. If we try to think of this

© Africa Studio/Shutterstock.com

from a parent's perspective, we could see that a parent may not easily understand when educators talk to them in acronyms and jargon. For example, a parent may easily be confused if they heard a statement such as this:

> "Your child's IEP meeting will be held in the SPED room on May 2nd. We will send you a PWN. Please sign and return it. We will begin by discussing FERPA and FAPE. Then we will discuss his IEE in terms of his PLAFF and try to determine the LRE for him. He may need an OT/PT or even AT and may be served at a SDC or RSP. However, your input will help us determine the most effective goals, accommodations, and modifications to achieve the best results for your child."

Can you imagine being a parent and hearing all these acronyms and jargon? It would certainly be enough to intimidate a parent and make him or her feel inadequate when asked to add to the conversation. One way educators can encourage parents to participate in the process is to intentionally choose to talk without using the special education acronyms and jargon until the parent understands what the acronyms and jargon represent and mean. It may also be helpful to provide a list of acronyms at the first IEP meeting.

Other terms that may cause confusion deal with placement. There are many options available for student placement, and parents may not fully understand the meaning of words such as self-contained, inclusion, resource room, mainstreaming, special education local plan area, resource specialist program, and least restrictive environment. When talking with parents, it is important to ensure that they understand the environment recommended for their child; you can help by explaining the environment and how it differs from the general education classroom.

Cultural Barriers

Cultural barriers can be an extreme hindrance to a child's education. As a first-year second-grade teacher, I had 22 English-speaking students and one Spanish-speaking student in my class. The Spanish-speaking student did not speak or understand the English language, and I only knew a few words of Spanish. We had an immediate and intense communication barrier. If this were the situation in your classroom, what would be the first question you would ask yourself? The first question I asked myself was, "What in the world am I going to do to teach this one Spanish-speaking student at the same time I need to teach the other 22 students?" A multitude of other questions followed.

What will he do while I teach the other 22 students?
What will they do when I teach him?
Will he understand anything other than a smile?
Will he make friends?
How will he make friends?
What about my other students' test scores and grades?
Will their grades suffer because of time I need to spend with him?
Will his education suffer because of the time I need to spend with the other 22-students?
What resources does our school have?
Ultimately, all of these questions boil down to, "How can I provide the best education to meet this student's unique needs?"

The first step in determining how to help when cultural barriers exist is to examine our own **culturally responsive practices**. Do we practice cultural humility, or do we practice (even if unintended) cultural superiority? Practicing cultural humility allows us to "overcome the natural tendency to view one's own beliefs, values, and worldview as superior, and instead be open to the beliefs, values, and worldview of the [culturally and linguistically diverse parent]" (Hook, Davis, Owen, Worthington, & Utsey, 2013, p. 354). This means we should try to understand the family as much as possible, from their perspective, rather than projecting our cultural influences on them.

After we have examined our own culturally responsive practices, we need to determine the best course of action. This may be very similar to the way we would handle other IEPs. For example, we would start with the PLAFF and proceed from that point. Since this student's needs involve a cultural barrier, it may be that the parents will have a similar barrier to the child's; this may require an interpreter. Again, each situation is unique and needs to be handled and decided as a unique situation.

Logistical Problems

Logistical barriers may simply be a matter of the parents not being able to make arrangements to be at the meeting. For example, a parent may work at a job that makes it nearly impossible for him or her to take a day off from work to attend a meeting. Additionally, the parent may prefer not to bring their other children to the IEP meeting but may be unable to secure child care. Parents may be divorced and may prefer not to work together. There may also be a language barrier which inhibits effective communication. There are a multitude of logistical reasons that may deter a parent from attending an IEP meeting. It is important to encourage the parents to participate but not to make assumptions about their lack of involvement should they not participate.

All these logistical reasons may cause parents to feel inferior, and thus not feel as eager to participate in the IEP process. Though educators may know more about teaching students, they typically do not know the whole child as well as the parent does. Parents have the privilege of knowing their child in ways that people outside of the family may likely never know unless they are told. For example, my son is a 16-year-old, 240-pound sophomore football player who also has attention-deficit hyperactivity disorder. To most teachers, he appears to be somewhat disrespectful, aloof, and not necessarily as bright as many kids in the class. However, there are two very critical pieces of information that would change his teacher's perception of him, if they knew. The first is that he learns by doing and not by listening and reading. He is border-line brilliant (spoken like a true mom) when it comes to making music digitally, but none of his teachers know this about him. If his teachers knew, and applied it to his learning, he would be able to learn and express his knowledge in a way that builds on his strength rather than his weaknesses. The other piece of information that is important is that he is an auditory learner. That being the case, he does not need to take notes like other students. As a matter of fact, he has specifically said to me, "Mom I can either listen to the teacher and learn, or I can take notes and turn them in for a grade, but I will not learn anything if I have to do that." A few of his teachers have been insistent that he takes notes, despite being told this information. Perhaps that is because they learn best by taking notes. Personally, I take notes to learn. I am a writer, and if I do not take notes, I typically do not remember. However, the opposite is true for my son. If he takes notes, rather than listen, he will not learn. Teachers must understand the significance of this. All students are different, and they will be different types of learners than the teacher. It is the teacher's responsibility to adjust to the learner, and not the other way around.

> *All students are different, and on many occasions, will be a different type of learner than the teacher. It is the teacher's responsibility to adjust to the learner, and not the other way around.*

Conclusion

Parents have incredible insight, and an effective teacher will aggressively seek information from parents and use it to benefit the student. Most kids act one way at home and to some degree, another way at school. As an educator, it is important for you to know and apply the law to all situations involving parents; this will help ensure that their legal rights are not violated. Additionally, in order to have the most effective educational situation for the student, the educator must remove as many barriers to parental participation as possible. Having both the parental and teacher voices represented in an IEP meeting will allow the team to work together using as many sides of the story as possible to determine the best educational goals and outcomes for the student. Remember the words of Proverbs 31:8 which say, "Speak out on behalf of the voiceless, and for the rights of all who are vulnerable" (Common English Bible).

Chapter Highlights

In 1975, parents were given the role of team members and decision-makers regarding the education of their child in the Education of All Handicapped Children Act, which is known today as Individuals with Disabilities Education Act (IDEA).

Since parents play an instrumental role in developing an IEP, and are required team members, reaching out to them and making them feel wanted and included is an essential element of the Christian educator's role.

In cases of divorce, the courts determine which parent has legal authority to make educational decisions.

Custody documents typically state which parent(s) have the legal right to make decisions regarding the child's education, and to what extent those decisions can be made if both parents do have a voice in those decisions.

According to IDEA, if a court order designates a specific person as the educational decision-maker, that person has the rights of the parent (34 C.F.R. § 300.30[b][2]).

Some of the most successful IEP meetings are the ones where the team leader is able to draw on every participant's strengths and mesh that information into one cohesive, beneficial document aimed at helping the student meet his or her fullest potential.

Educators and parents need to understand the legal rights governing the IEP process regarding parents in order to make decisions that abide by the law and are in the best interest of the child.

According to IDEA, parents of a child with a disability have the right:

> To examine all records relating to such child and to participate in meetings with respect to the identification, evaluation, and educational placement of the child, and the provision of a free appropriate public education to such child, and to obtain independent educational evaluation of the child (20.U.S.C. §1415[b][1]).

Parents must be formally given written notice prior to an IEP meeting.

When we have high expectations for our students, they tend to live up to that expectation. The opposite is also true.

Parents should be encouraged to attend school events and events in the community.

One way educators can encourage parents to participate in the process is to intentionally choose to talk without using the special education acronyms and jargon until the parent understands what the acronyms and jargon represent and mean.

Practicing cultural humility allows us to "overcome the natural tendency to view one's own beliefs, values, and worldview as superior, and instead be open to the beliefs, values, and worldview of the [culturally and linguistically diverse parent]" (Hook, Davis, Owen, Worthington, & Utsey, 2013, p. 354).

All students are different, and they will be different types of learners than the teacher. It is the teacher's responsibility to adjust to the learner, and not the other way around.

Chapter Review Questions

1. In your own words, write a definition of "parent" that accurately reflects the definition in IDEA.
2. When a student has anything other than two biological, married parents, what is your responsibility as the teacher?
3. What are some ways Romans 12:3b-4 applies to an educator's leadership role in the IEP process? Use examples and identify at least two other verses that could also apply to the IEP process.
4. What are parents' rights when they have a child with disabilities according to IDEA, and what are some ways you can ensure those rights are upheld?
5. Describe the different relationships in the IEP process, and explain the significance of each of those relationships. Write an example of a possible IEP participant list. (Ensure all required participants are included.)
6. Identify the elements of FAPE and the importance of each of those elements.
7. If a parent asked you what would be the best way for his or her student to learn at home, how would you respond?
8. What are the primary benefits and barriers to parental participation in the IEP process? What are some possible solutions you could recommend for those barriers?

Additional Resources

- For an example letter for requesting an evaluation visit this website: http://www.ldonline.org/article/14620
- For a list of benefits of parental involvement in the IEP process visit this website: https://www.education.com/reference/article/benefits-parent-involvement-research/

References

American Psychological Association (APA). (2017). Marriage & divorce. *APA*. Retrieved from http://www.apa.org/topics/divorce/

Blue-Banning, M., Summers, J. A., Frankland, H. C., Nelson, L. L., & Beegle, G. (2004). Dimensions of family and professional partnerships: Constructive guidelines for collaboration. *Exceptional Children*, *70*(2), 167–184. doi:10.1177/001440290407000203

Haines, S. J., Gross, J. M. S., Blue-Banning, M., Francis, G. L., & Turnbull, A. P. (2015). Fostering family-school and community-school partnerships in inclusive schools: Using practice as a guide. *Research and Practice for Persons with Severe Disabilities*, *40*(3), 227–239. doi:10.1177/1540796915594141

Henderson, A. T., & Berla, N. (1994). *A new generation of evidence: The family is critical to student achievement.* Columbia, MD: National Committee for Citizens in Education.

Hook, J. N., Davis, D. E., Owen, J., Worthington, E. L., Jr., & Utsey, S. O. (2013). Cultural humility: Measuring openness to culturally diverse clients. *Journal of Counseling Psychology*, *60*(3), 353–366. doi:10.1037/a0032595

Individuals with Disabilities Education Improvement Act of 2004. 20 U.S.C. § 1400 *et seq.*

Losinski, M., Katsiyannis, A., White, S., & Wiseman, N. (2015). Who is the parent? Guidance from case law on parental participation in the IEP process. *Teaching Exceptional Children*, *48*(3), 144–150. doi:10.1177/0040059915605800

Namkung, E. H., Song, J., Greenberg, J. S., Mailick, M. R., & Floyd, F. J. (2015). The relative risk of divorce in parents of children with developmental disabilities: Impacts of lifelong parenting. *American Journal of Intellectual and Developmental Disabilities*, *120(*6), 514–526. doi:10.1352/1944-7558-120.6.514.

Rodriguez, R. J., Blatz, E. T., & Elbaum, B. (2014). Strategies to involve families of Latino students with disabilities: When parent initiative is not enough. *Intervention in School and Clinic*, *49*(5), 263–270. doi:10.1177/1053451213513956

Rusu, I., & Weisman, R. (2015). The impact of individualized education programs on free appropriate public education. *Journal of the American Academy of Psychiatry and the Law*, *43*(2), 253–255.

Turnbull, A. A., Turnbull, H. R., Erwin, E. J., Soodak, L. C., & Shogren, K. A. (2010). *Families, professionals, and exceptionality: Positive outcomes through partnership and trust* (6th ed.). Boston, MA: Pearson.

Woodworth, J. (2016). IEPs, 504 plans and behavior contracts. *The Exceptional Parent (Online)*, 46(9), 54–56.

CHAPTER 3

Present Level of Academic Achievement and Functional Performance

Learning Outcomes

After reading this chapter, you should be able to:

- ❏ Identify the three required elements in a PLAAFP
- ❏ Define academic achievement and provide relevant examples
- ❏ Define functional performance skills and provide relevant examples
- ❏ Differentiate between formal and informal assessments
- ❏ Explain the significance of building an IEP in terms of a biblical foundation

Vocabulary

- ❏ PLAAFP
- ❏ Academic Achievement
- ❏ Functional Performance
- ❏ Formal Assessments
- ❏ Informal Assessments

Present Level of Academic Achievement and Functional Performance

Individuals with Disabilities Education Act (IDEA) requires that schools conduct a complete and individual initial evaluation to determine if a student has a disability and to determine the student's educational needs (20 U.S.C. § 1414 [a][1][C][i]). An Individualized Education Plan (IEP) must be fully developed to offer the student an opportunity to make progress in all relevant domains. It is through a complete and individualized assessment of all of a student's needs that these domains are identified and addressed in the IEP. Prior to beginning the Present Level of Academic Achievement and Functional Performance (PLAAFP) section of the IEP, the IEP team leader must confirm that all necessary assessments were conducted during the evaluation process. To the degree that a student's assessment is inadequate or inaccurate, the student's IEP will also be inadequate and inaccurate (Bateman, 2011).

The first major step in the IEP process is completing the student's **PLAAFP**. This information lays the foundation for developing reasonable annual goals and services for the student with special needs and serves to guide the expectations for student progress for the upcoming school year. If all of the student's needs identified by the assessments are not included in the PLAAFP section, it is likely that the student's right to Free Appropriate Public Education may have been denied. Additionally, incomplete or insufficiently prepared PLAAFPs will hinder the student's academic achievement, as the information needed for educational decision-making will not be available. "The IEP must stand solidly and squarely on a foundation of current, accurate assessments of the level of performance in academic and functional areas" (Bateman, 2011, p. 96), as this will provide the IEP team with the information necessary to build an IEP with a solid foundation.

Since the PLAAFP is the first step in the IEP process, it should be considered the foundation of the IEP. Proverbs 3:19 says, "By wisdom the Lord laid the earth's foundations, by understanding he set the heavens in place." When we examine this verse, and consider the task before us, we need to focus on two very important words from this verse: wisdom and understanding. In the process of building a PLAAFP, how do we gain wisdom and understanding? As Christians, we are taught in the Bible that wisdom and understanding come from the Lord (Exodus 31:3, 1 Kings 4:29, 1 Kings 10:24). Building the foundation of the IEP documents will require both wisdom and understanding, so it is essential that we seek the Lord; thus, praying should be a consistent part of the IEP process for the Christian teacher, as this is how wisdom and understanding are gained.

Why is this important? In a parable about building your life on Christ, the Bible says, "The rain came down, the streams rose, and the winds blew and beat against that house; yet it did not fall, because it had its foundation on the rock" (Matthew 7:25). This verse refers to Christians building their lives on Christ, our solid foundation. What if we took that parable and applied the wisdom to the PLAAFP? The information in the PLAAFP will serve as the foundation of all educational decisions made for an entire year for a student; therefore, it is critical that this information be thorough and accurate.

In this book, we are going to write an IEP, including all of the critical components, from start to finish. This IEP will be about a ninth grade student named Brett Smith. Brett has a disability, and we are going to work hard to write an IEP that will support him in his educational journey throughout his ninth grade school year. We will begin with the IEP Cover Page.

Cover Page

Before we get started with the PLAAFP, let us begin by viewing the Cover Page of the IEP. This page is meant to offer a quick snapshot of information pertaining to the student and the IEP team.

Liberty Academic School
XXXX XXXX XXXXXX
XXXXXXX XXXXXX
XXXXXXX XXXXXX
Telephone: XXXXXX
Fax: XXXXXXXXXX
Email: xxxxx@xxxx.com
Website: www.xxxxxxx.com

Individualized Education Plan
Cover Page

Student Name: Brett Smith Date: 9/20/22

Disability: Specific Learning Disability and Attention Deficit Hyperactivity Disorder

Grade: 9 DOB: 3/24/07 Age: 15

Parent/Guardian Name: David & Mary Smith

Street Address: 1101 First Street

City: Majestic State: VA Zip Code: 12345

Phone #: (123)456-7890

A copy of the IEP was given to the parent/guardian/student by: Kelly Garman

IEP Team Leader: Kelly Garman Phone #: (111)-111-1111

The IEP that accompanies this document is meant to support the positive process and team approach. The IEP is a working document that outlines the vision for the student's future and includes the student's strengths and needs.

IEP Summary Information	
Projected IEP Start Date:	9/30/22
Projected IEP End Date:	6/24/23
Projected Annual Review Date:	6/24/23
Projected Date for Reevaluation:	6/24/25
Extended School Services	No
Behavior Intervention Plan	Yes
Supplementary Aids and Services	Yes
Assistive Technology	No
Supports for School Personnel	No
Testing Accommodations	Yes
Participate in State/District Assessments	Yes
Special Transportation	No

Participants Involved

The list below indicates that the individual participated in the development of the IEP and the decisions regarding placement. Participation does not authorize consent. Parent consent (or student if 18+ years of age) is indicated on the "Prior Notice" page.

Name of Participant	Position
David & Mary Smith	Father and Mother
Brett Smith	Student
Shonda Miller	Administrator
Kelly Garman	Special Education Teacher, Team Leader
Stuart Fisher	General Education Teacher
Dr. Nathaniel Salinas	Guidance Counselor
Russ Greer	Speech/Language Therapist

The information on the Cover Page serves as a quick reference to identify the student, parents, and team members. It also discloses important dates that all team members need to be cognizant of such as the most recent eligibility and re-evaluation dates, as well as the date of the IEP meeting. The form above is just a sample, and almost every state and district will have a similar, but unique cover page. The next page that needs to be filled out contains factors that the IEP team needs to be aware of in order to make decisions regarding the student's educational needs.

Factors for IEP Team Consideration

This document is intended to convey information that will be used on the PLAAFP that all team members need to consider. Not all states and districts will have this document; however, this information should be included on the PLAAFP if it is not included here, as this information should guide decisions made for the student.

The questions on this document should be answered in shorter answers than the answers on the PLAAFP. For example, the first question requires the results of the initial or most recent evaluation(s) of the student. This could be a diagnosis or an evaluation from a doctor or specialist. Including the strengths of the student is important since strengths should be used to enhance learning and support weaknesses. The third question refers to the academic, developmental, and functional needs of the student. Again, this can be somewhat concise here, since it will be elaborated on in the PLAAFP. Including a section specifically for parental input is important, as this allows all teams members to hear the voices of the parents; this information is critical for all team members to be aware of, especially in the IEP meeting. When team members understand the desire of the parents, it allows team members to help meet the parent's expectations or to come to the meeting prepared to help the parents understand a different perspective if that is what the team members believe is best for the student. The fifth question addresses the communication needs of the student. Does the student struggle with communication? If so, how? In the next chapter, we will discuss benchmarks and short-term objectives, but the sixth question is asking if this student has a need for them.

Liberty Academic School
XXXX XXXX XXXXXX
XXXXXXX XXXXXX
XXXXXXX XXXXXX

Telephone: XXXXXX
Fax: XXXXXXXXXX
Email: xxxxx@xxxx.com
Website: www.xxxxxxx.com

Individualized Education Plan
Summary of Performance
Factors for IEP Team Consideration

Student Name: Brett Smith Date: 9/7/22

Disability: Specific Learning Disability and Attention Deficit Hyperactivity Disorder

DOB: 3/24/07 Age: 15 Grade: 9

IEP Team Manager: Kelly Garman

The following information should be considered by the IEP team in regards to educational decisions made for the student, as it serves as a summary of the student's performance. Please see other sections of the IEP, as noted, for more precise details concerning specific areas of learning for this student.

1. Summary of Academic Achievement:

Include results of the initial or most recent evaluation of this student.

Cognitive testing indicates overall cognitive functioning in the borderline range with a Full-Scale IQ of 73 SS. Verbal Comprehension (73 SS) skills increased from the previous evaluation (65 SS) and is in the borderline range, along with Perceptual Reasoning (78 SS).

Mathematics

Numerical Operations (72 SS) is in the borderline range. Significant deficits are noted in math Problem-Solving (59 SS). Inconsistent focused attention was noted during testing. For example, Brett was redirected three times based on lack of answering questions while looking away from the test and tapping his pencil. Additionally, Brett asked to get water twice and to stand up to work once. Brett's core math skills are significantly below grade level.

In the resource classroom, he struggles with equations, computation, and multistep word problems.

Reading/Written Language

Speech and language reevaluation reveals a Core Language score (76 SS) in the borderline range; however, significant improvement is noted from previous test score (61SS). During his twice-weekly 30-min speech/language therapy sessions, Brett exhibits effort on a mostly consistent basis. The speech/language pathologist noted improvements in verbal comprehension based on test scores 73 (SS) and improved participation based on teacher observation. Brett continues to work on soliciting additional info or asking for repetition when unsure.

Reading comprehension skills (94 SS) and decoding skills (93 SS) are in the average range. He can decode and answer basic comprehension questions. Long-term retention of material is an area of concern. Word reading (75 SS) is in the borderline range. Significant deficits are noted in listening comprehension (60 SS). Effort was inconsistent during testing. For example, Brett asked random off-topic questions and was redirected by the teacher twice.

Additionally, shortly after Brett began reading the third section of the reading comprehension section, he put his head down on the desk to take a break twice.

In the resource room, Brett consistently uses reading strategies and refers back to the text to assist with comprehension. Assistance is required with higher-order thinking skills. A graphic organizer is used for writing grammar. Mechanics are weak based on writing samples (documents included in the IEP as evidence).

2. Strengths of the student:

Brett is highly motivated and gets along well with others. Though he benefits from working in a small group setting for his academics, he also enjoys social interaction in a large group setting. Brett is also motivated by information pertaining to automobiles.

3. Summary of Functional Performance, as applicable:

Behavior scales indicate a few conduct issues. Progress is hindered by lack of attention and concentration. Brett demonstrates weak organizational skills and does not complete assignments and homework in a timely manner. He requires consistent teacher support to accomplish his work accurately and in a timely manner. His parents indicate that Brett is on medication for Attention Deficit Hyperactivity Disorder (ADHD) and for tics. Stress increases his tics.

4. Summary of Transition: Postsecondary Goals, as applicable:

According to his parents, David and Mary, Brett's interests are in video games, cars, and sports (soccer, football, basketball) but his desire is to become an auto mechanic.

Career Cluster Interest Survey reveals career interests in the areas of Information Technology, Science/Technology/Engineering, and Marketing. CITE Learning Styles Instrument indicates five areas of major learning preference: Auditory/Numerical, Auditory/Language, Auditory/ Visual/Kinesthetic, Social/Group, and Expressive/Oral.

5. Parental concerns for enhancing the student's education:

David and Mary are concerned that Brett's math skills may hinder him from achieving his post-secondary goals. Although he has made some progress for the past few years, they want him to be on track to finish high school on grade-level in math, as well as in all academic areas.

6. Communication needs of the student:

Brett continues to work on asking for additional help when he needs further clarification on a concept or problem. He needs to be a stronger self-advocate when it comes to asking for assistance. His is working on this skill with his speech/language pathologist.

7. Need for benchmarks or short-term objectives:

Brett needs to be assessed quarterly in the content areas in order to measure progress. He will take the state end-of-subject and/or end of grade tests and local benchmark tests at regular intervals along with grade-level peers with appropriate accommodations to measure his progress against state and local standards. He also needs to have measurable short-term objectives for reading, writing, and math.

8. Does the student require an Assistive Technology device and/or service?

Yes or No (circle one)

If yes, does the committee recommend the device(s) be used in the student's home?

Yes or No (circle one)

9. Does the student need strategies, including behavioral interventions, supports, and other strategies to address behaviors that impede the student's learning or that of others?

Yes or No (circle one)

If yes, does the student need a behavioral intervention plan?

Yes or No (circle one)

10. In the case of a student with limited English proficiency, does he/she need special education services to address his/her language needs as they relate to the IEP?

Yes or No or Not Applicable (circle one)

11. In the case of a student who is blind or is visually impaired, the IEP team must provide for instruction or use of Braille, if assessment results indicate need. When considering that Braille is not appropriate for the child, the IEP team may use the Functional Vision and Learning Media Assessment for Students who are Pre-Academic or Academic and Visually Impaired in Grades K-12 (FVLMA) or similar instrument.

Does this student need instruction in Braille or use of Braille?

Yes or No or Not Applicable (circle one)

12. In the case of a student who is deaf or hard of hearing, consider the student's language and communication needs, opportunities for direct communications with peers and professional personnel in the student's language and communication mode, academic level, and full range of needs, including opportunities for direct instruction in the student's language and communication mode.

Does this student need a particular device or service to address his/her communication needs?

Yes or No or Not Applicable (circle one)

13. Extended School Year (ESY)

Does this student require extended school year services?

Yes or No (circle one)

What Is Included in the PLAAFP?

PLAAFP statements must include the student's current performance level as well as how the student's disability impacts access to the general education curriculum. This information informs the IEP team about the student's needs so that team members can complete the remainder of the IEP form using this much-needed information. When the PLAAFP is written with substantial detail, the IEP team members will be able to measure the student's progress as the PLAAFP may serve as baseline data. Essentially, there are three specific elements that must be addressed in great detail in the PLAAFP:

1. The students' PLAAFP
2. The impact of the disability on the student's ability to progress in the general education curriculum
3. The students' needs resulting from the disability

Where Do We Get the Information for the PLAAFP?

PLAAFP information is derived from formal and informal assessments including assessments conducted by the IEP team, from documented progress made on previous IEP goals, and from documented performance on grade-level curriculum standards. To begin, it will be helpful to clearly define what is meant by academic achievement and functional performance, as these are two elements of the PLAAFP that can easily be confused, if not properly defined.

© Andrey_Popov/Shutterstock.com

Academic Achievement

Academic achievement generally refers to a child's performance in academic areas. For example, math is considered an academic area, whereas cooking skills are not considered academic. Think of academic achievement as including academic subjects such as math, reading, language, arts, social studies, science, history, language arts, etc. For preschool children, academic achievement refers to age-appropriate developmental levels.

© F8 studio/Shutterstock.com

Functional Performance

Functional performance generally refers to skills or activities that may not be considered academic or related to a child's academic achievement. Functional achievement is often used in the context of routine activities of everyday living and is varied depending on the individual needs of the child. For example, functional skills would include personal hygiene (brushing teeth, bathing), cooking (preparing healthy meals), housekeeping skills (washing laundry, making a bed), transportation for older students (riding a bus or driving a vehicle), job training skills, and more. Functional performance can have a major impact on educational achievement.

Academic achievement and functional performance must both be addressed in the PLAAFP; the state standards must also be addressed. After the next few paragraphs is a sample PLAAFP, but is it not the only example that you may come across. Many states and districts have their own IEP forms that must be utilized, but the required information contained in each section should be the same.

Summary of Academic Achievement

In order to complete the first section of the PLAAFP on Academic Achievement, both formal and informal assessments must be included. Strengths and limitations of the student should be stated in terms of the grade-level state standards. It is tempting to only include limitations, as that is what is typically addressed. However, noting a student's strengths may help the IEP team determine how to address a student's limitations by using the student's strengths to build up or improve the weak areas.

Formal assessments are an important part of this section. **Formal assessments** include standardized tests, intelligence tests, and cognitive tests. These tests are norm-referenced, which means that they compare a student's performance to similar populations with an appropriate comparison group (e.g., those of the same age group, sex, education level, and/or race/ethnicity).

Intelligence tests provide an IQ score and measure a student's ability to process information. Cognitive tests, which are also standardized, may include the *Wechsler Intelligence Scales for Children*, the *Stanford Binet Intelligence Scales*, or others. Achievement tests may include the *Woodcock Johnson Psychoeducational Battery*, the *Kaufman Test of Educational Achievement*, or others.

Informal assessments may include various and detailed information, and that information may be obtained through checklists, observational antidotes, student work samples, curriculum-based assessment, teacher made tests, and criterion referenced tests such as the *Dynamic Indicators of Basic Early Literacy Skills* (DIBELS) and the *Brilliance Comprehensive Inventory of Basic Skills*. Other informal assessments may include parental input/concerns, progress toward last year's goals, input from service providers, and information from the student such as post-high school goals.

Summary of Functional Performance

Informal and formal assessments are also used to provide information about a student's functional performance. Formal assessments of the student's functional skills may include state or district-provided alternative assessments specifically designed for students with cognitive disabilities or criterion-referenced test such as *The Checklist of Adaptive Living Skills* or *The Brigance Diagnostic Inventory of Early Development*. Informal assessments of functional performance may include a checklist of skills that indicates what the student is able and not able to accomplish.

The IEP focuses on access to, and success in, the general education curriculum. Again, remember that the PLAAFP must include:

1. The students' PLAAFP
2. The impact of the disability on the student's ability to progress in the general education curriculum
3. The student's needs resulting from the disability

Now that we have detailed the PLAAFP, let us look at an example of one.

Liberty Academic School
XXXX XXXX XXXXXX
XXXXXXX XXXXXX
XXXXXXX XXXXXX

Telephone: XXXXXX
Fax: XXXXXXXXXX
Email: xxxxx@xxxx.com
Website: www.xxxxxxx.com

Individualized Education Plan
Present Level of Academic Achievement and Functional Performance (PLAAFP)

Student Name: Brett Smith   Meeting Date: 9/20/22

Student Strengths, Preferences, and Interests:

- Brett's strength is that he is motivated to learn and helpful to the teacher and his peers.
- His interests are in video games, cars, and sports (soccer, football, basketball). He will occasionally check out a book from the library on hot rod cars or how to build engines.
- According to the CITE Learning Styles Instrument, Brett prefers five areas of major learning: Auditory/Numerical, Auditory/Language, Auditory/Visual/Kinesthetic, Social/Group, and Expressive/Oral.
- Cluster Interest Survey reveals career interests in the areas of Information Technology, Science/Technology/Engineering, and Marketing.

Assessment/Evaluation Data:

Evaluation/Reports Included:

Parent Report and Observations (01/31/21)
Speech/Language Re-evaluation (01//11/21)
Speech/Language Progress Summary (01/15/2021)
Guidance Report (01/31/21)
Teacher Progress Summary (01/31/21)
Educational Evaluation (01/12/21)

Test Results:

WIAT—III (01/12/21)
Basic Reading 84 (Standard Score), 14 (Percentile Rank)
Essay Comp: Grammar & Mechanics 82 (SS), 10 (PR)
Essay Composition 77 (SS), 5 (PR)
Expressive Vocabulary 74 (SS), 4 (PR)
Listening Comprehension 60 (SS), 0.3 (PR)
Oral Discourse Comprehension 56 (SS), 0.2 (PR)
Oral Expression 87 (SS), 19 (PR)

Oral Language 70 (SS), 2 (PR)
Oral Reading Accuracy 75 (SS), 5 (PR)
Oral Reading Fluency 82 (SS), 13 (PR)
Oral Reading Rate 84 (SS), 14 (PR)
Oral Word Fluency 96 (SS), 38 (PR)

Reading Comprehension 93 (SS), 32 (PR)
Receptive Vocabulary 92 (SS), 3 (PR)
Sentence Building 74 (SS), 4 (PR)
Sentence Combining 84 (SS), 14 (PR)
Sentence Composition 78 (SS), 7 (PR)
Sentence Repetition 100 (SS), 50 (PR)
Spelling 80 (SS), 9 (PR)
Theme Development and Text Organization 67 (SS), 1 (PR)
Total Achievement 71 (SS), 3 (PR)
Total Reading 82 (SS), 12 (PR)
Word Count 89 (SS), 23 (PR)
Word Reading 75 (SS), 5 (PR)
Written Expression 74 (SS), 4 (PR)
Math Fluency—Addition 83 (SS), 14 (PR)
Math Fluency—Subtraction 86 (SS), 18 (PR)
Math Fluency—Multiplication 71 (SS), 3 (PR)
Math Problem Solving 60 (SS), 0.4 (PR)
Mathematics 66 (SS), 1 (PR)
Numerical Operations 72 (SS), 3 (PR)
Math Fluency 78 (SS), 7 (PR)

Wechsler Abbreviated Scale of Intelligence-II
Full Scale IQ 73 (SS), 5 (PR)
Perceptual Reasoning 78 (SS), 7 (PR)
Verbal Comprehension 73 (SS), 4 (PR)

CELF-5
Core Language Score 76 (SS), 5 (PR)
Formulated Sentences 6 (SS), 9 (PR)
Recalling Sentences 8 (SS), 25 (PR)
Semantic Relationships 5 (SS), 5 (PR)
Understanding Spoken Paragraphs 5 (SS), 5 (PR)

State and District-wide Assessments:
None

Current Student Academic Performance:

Writing:
Brett's writing skills are progressing slowly. The writing process is hindered by his lack of ability to maintain focus. He can generate ideas for writing, but he needs assistance to include sufficient details. Graphic organizers and outlines support his writing, and one must still be provided for him in most instances. Essays pose a significant problem for Brett due to the number of organizational elements required for success. His grammar and mechanics skills are below grade-level. When prompted to write about a topic related to his required reading, such as a book report or essay, Brett struggles due to reading comprehension difficulties and his ability to organize his thoughts into a coherent essay.

Reading:
Brett is able to answer basic knowledge questions when reading at his independent level. He has difficulty with questions that require higher-order thinking skills, context clues, and determining the meaning of unfamiliar words. He also struggles with drawing conclusions and making inferences, which negatively impacts his comprehension and retention when reading from grade-level textbooks. Specific reading strategies such as

re-reading the text, self-question, and summarizing his understanding of the text have helped, but he is hesitant to use these strategies unless prompted. He does not independently use details to answer questions accurately and to support his inferences and ideas. At times, his inability to stay focused impacts his ability to understand and retain information. Speech/Language: Brett is a considerate, respectful, and typically engaged student. His attention issues present a challenge quite often, but he responds when redirected. Brett is able to participate in conversational dialogue, but he is negatively impacted by language processing and auditory memory problems. He frequently demonstrates difficulty with higher-order questions and organizing sentences when incorporating abstract ideas, but is able to use basic communication skills. Brett has been working on strategies to improve his word retrieval and auditory memory skills, but he continues to struggle. Brett's articulation is characterized by a distortion of the /p/ phoneme in many positions of words and blends. Math: When he is feeling confident, Brett works diligently to complete his assignments. However, he benefits from constant support and reinforcement as well as the use of a calculator. He has difficulty learning grade-level math concepts, and he is most successful in a small group or one-to-one setting. He can follow one-step procedures, but he has difficulty with multiple-step problems and simple computation. Even after extensive modeling and guided practice, Brett requires support to accurately follow mathematical procedures and solve problems. He also has a hard time remembering and applying concepts over time, which makes cumulative math exams extremely challenging.
Effects of Disability on General Curriculum: Describe the effect of student needs on progress in the general curriculum or, for a preschool student, effect of student needs on participation in appropriate activities. Writing: Brett needs to include sufficient details in his writing to support ideas and inferences and utilize a standard format to organize required elements of an essay. Proofreading and checking his writing for grammar and mechanics need to be a consistent part of his writing routine. Reading: Brett needs to develop his comprehension of content material. He needs to develop his ability to answer questions requiring higher-order thinking skills. He needs to use context clues to determine the meaning of unknown words. Speech/Language: Brett needs to develop language processing, verbal/written expression, auditory memory, and word retrieval skills. Therapist support is needed in order to monitor his articulation of the /p/ phoneme in structured speech and spontaneous conversation. Math: Brett needs to improve his recall of basic facts and accuracy of computation. He requires direct support to learn and practice grade-level math skills. He struggles with multi-step procedures. A list of steps to follow from the beginning of a problem until the end increases his ability to succeed. Summary: Brett has a significant delay in written expression, language skills, speech skills, attention skills, math calculation, and math concepts which interferes with age-appropriate activities in the general education curriculum.

Current Student Functional Performance:
Social Competence: *Brett is helpful, cooperative, and friendly, which are skills that strengthen his social competence. His social and emotional levels are within age expectations. At times, Brett is quiet and withdrawn; this typically occurs when he is feeling stressed or lacking confidence in his ability. There are no social or emotional needs that require special education services at this time.* Physical Development: *Brett enjoys sports and participates in Physical Education class. Brett's diagnosed medical condition impacts his education. He is diagnosed with ADHD, Dysgraphia, and Transient Tic Disorder (involuntary tics). He exhibits symptoms of cognitive impulsivity, distractibility, and inattention. David, Brett's father, reports that Brett is exhausted from the school day and finds it exceptionally challenging for him to complete homework or study after school. He is on medication for ADHD and Transient Tic Disorder.* *Needs: Brett needs to continue to learn compensatory skills for the negative educational impact of his diagnosed ADHD.*
Based on Effects, Describe Deficits that Require Functional Support: *Brett needs a teacher-to-student ratio that is small. He needs frequent redirection to attend to tasks. Seating near the front of the room will minimize distractions and near the teacher will allow for frequent redirection and opportunities to check-in. Information should be taught sequentially with clear steps. He needs repetition and review of lessons as well as assistance with organizational skills and time management. He also craves social interaction, which may impact the least restrictive environment.*

Note the sections included and the wealth of information that is expected to be present. This information will serve as the foundation for the remaining critical decisions that need to be made regarding this student. Without this information, the IEP team does not have much information to base their decisions on, which is why this is such an important part of the IEP process.

Notice that the PLAAFP statements above include all of the required elements. The student's strengths and weaknesses are noted for both the academic achievement and functional achievements, the impact that each student's disability has on his or her ability to progress in the general education curriculum is included, and the needs resulting from the disability are written.

Conclusion

It requires a substantial amount of time to correctly and thoroughly complete the PLAAFP. Time spent on building this foundation will help educators, as well as the student, to reap rewards as the year progresses. For educators, having all of the information required to make an informed decision regarding the student in one location will save a lot of time as the year progresses. The teacher will not have to look for past assessment information or progress because time will have been well spent building this foundation at the beginning of the school year. Additionally, the PLAAFP will serve as baseline data throughout the school year, and it will be referred to often to monitor and record progress. For the student, a well-developed PLAAFP will help to ensure that the IEP team members responsible for educational decision-making are fully informed about the students' present strengths and weaknesses as well as the specific needs regarding the general education curriculum. For the Christian educator, consider this verse, Luke 6:49:

> But the one who hears my words and does not put them into practice is like a man who built a house on the ground without a foundation. The moment the torrent struck that house, it collapsed and its destruction was complete.

Trials will come in the IEP process. For the team leader who has built the PLAAFP on a solid foundation of data, evidence, and assessments, that foundation will hold firm. Effective decisions will be made based on this solid information, and the student will be the ultimate beneficiary.

Chapter Highlights

IDEA requires that schools conduct a complete and individual initial evaluation to determine if a student has a disability and to determine the student's educational needs (20 U.S.C. § 1414 [a][1][C][i]).

The first major step in the IEP process is completing the student's **PLAAFP**.

"The IEP must stand solidly and squarely on a foundation of current, accurate assessments of the level of performance in academic and functional areas" (Bateman, 2011, p. 96), as this will provide the IEP team with the information necessary to build an IEP with a solid foundation.

Building the foundation of the IEP documents will require both wisdom and understanding, so it is essential that we seek the Lord; thus, praying should be a consistent part of the IEP process for the Christian teacher, as this is how wisdom and understanding are gained.

PLAAFP statements must include the student's current performance level as well as how the student's disability impacts access to the general education curriculum.

PLAAFP information is derived from formal and informal assessments including assessments conducted by the IEP team, from documented progress made on previous IEP goals, and from documented performance on grade-level curriculum standards.

Functional performance generally refers to skills or activities that may not be considered academic or related to a child's academic achievement. Functional achievement is often used in the context of routine activities of everyday living and is varied depending on the individual needs of the child.

Academic achievement and functional performance must both be addressed in the PLAAFP; the state standards must also be addressed.

Formal assessments include standardized tests, intelligence tests, and cognitive tests. These tests are norm-referenced, which means that they compare a student's performance to similar populations with an appropriate comparison group (e.g., those of the same age group, sex, education level, and/or race/ethnicity).

Informal assessments may include various and detailed information, and that information may be obtained through checklists, observational antidotes, student work samples, curriculum-based assessment, teacher made tests, and criterion referenced tests.

Chapter Review Questions

1. Use the PLAAFP examples from this chapter to write one academic goal and one functional/behavioral goal.
2. List and describe the three elements that are required in a PLAAFP.
3. Define academic achievement and identify one example from the PLAAFP examples above.
4. Define functional performance and identify an example from the PLAAFP examples above.
5. Write an example of an academic achievement and a functional performance other than those in the example above.
6. List five formal assessments and five informal assessments.
7. Why is it important to build a PLAAFP and IEP on a biblical foundation? Justify your answer using specific examples and scripture.

Additional Resources

Books

- *Starting with Their Strengths* by Deborah Lickey
- *A Measure of Success: The Influence of Curriculum-Based Measurement on Education* by Christine Espin

Websites

- For more information on the parental perspective of a PLAAFP visit this website: http://www.parentcenterhub.org/present-levels/
- For additional information on PLAAFP visit this website: http://www.parentcompanion.org/article/present-levels-of-academic-achievement-and-functional-performance-plaafp

References

Bateman, B. D. (2011). Individual education programs for children with disabilities. In J. M. Kauffman & D. P. Hallahan (Eds.), *Handbook of special education* (pp. 91–106). Philadelphia, PA: Taylor & Francis/ Routledge.

Individuals with Disabilities Education Improvement Act of 2004. 20 U.S.C., §§ 1400, et seq.

CHAPTER 4

Measurable Annual Goals

Learning Outcomes

After reading this chapter, you should be able to:

- ❑ Define Measurable Annual Goal
- ❑ Discuss why measurable goals are important and how they are used in the IEP process
- ❑ List the four required or standard elements of measurable annual goals
- ❑ Correctly write measurable annual goals
- ❑ Define Learning Objective
- ❑ List the three components of learning objectives
- ❑ Correctly write learning objectives
- ❑ Define Benchmarks
- ❑ Describe the differences between Measurable Annual Goals, Learning Objectives, and Benchmarks

Vocabulary

- ❑ Measurable Annual Goal
- ❑ Learning Objective
- ❑ Benchmarks

Measurable Annual Goals

The Present Levels of Academic Achievement and Functional Performance (PLAAFP) statements are the basis of the goals and services of an Individualized Education Plan (IEP), which is why building a solid foundation of information is critical to the student's educational success. The PLAAFP serves to inform the IEP team of the student's present abilities, including both strengths and weaknesses. This information will be used to design an educational program for the student with special needs. The purpose of the **measurable annual goals** is to provide a 12-month plan for the student's educational journey. If we look to the Bible for guidance, we find that Jeremiah 29:11 says, "'For I know the plans I have for you,' declares the Lord, 'plans to prosper you and not to harm you, plans to give you hope and a future'." This is exactly what the goals represent for our students; it is a plan to give them hope for their future.

marekuliasz/Shutterstock.com

Writing measurable annual goals is a critical component of the IEP, but in terms of the student's future, this is the plan for the next year of the student's life and must be given the attention that it deserves. My advice in the beginning of the book was to seek wisdom from the Lord throughout this journey, and with each significant milestone I would recommend that teachers make spending time with the Lord a priority. "Commit to the Lord whatever you do, and he will establish your plans" (Prov. 16:3). Before you begin the IEP process, and throughout the process of writing annual goals, I suggest that you seek the Lord's counsel. Ask Him what His plan is for this student and ask Him how you can be an integral part of His plan.

Team Approach

"Plans fail for lack of counsel, but with many advisers they succeed" (Prov. 15:22). This biblical wisdom, if adhered to, will be to the benefit of everyone on the team, but most importantly, it will benefit the student. In the first chapter, we listed the required team members as the parents, school administrator, special education teacher, general education teacher, service providers, specialists, and any other people who may lend to the Free Appropriate Public Education (FAPE) of the student. Though it may not be necessary to seek the input from all of these members for all goals, it would be wise to include the relevant person(s) for goals related to their area of expertise. For example, if one of the student's goals includes speech, it would seem wise to include the speech pathologist who will be working with the student. Collaborating with team members is the best way to share knowledge, practical experiences, and ideas to meet the student's educational needs. When team members work together, each member brings a unique set of gifts and talents that can be utilized to support student learning. As Paul wrote to the Romans:

> For as in one body we have many members, and the members do not all have the same function, so we, though many, are one body in Christ, and individually members one of another. Having gifts that differ according to the grace given to us, let us use them. (Rom. 12:4-6, English Standard Version)

This verse serves to further support the need to collaborate. The general education teacher does not have the same knowledge or experiences that the special education teacher has and vice versa. Both have the potential to convey valuable information that can make a tremendous difference in the life of the student. Oftentimes pride gets in the way of teachers sharing ideas and teaching responsibilities; this is always to the detriment of the student. "When pride comes, then comes disgrace, but with humility comes wisdom" (Prov. 11:2). Wisdom is what we need to influence others for eternity. I want to encourage you to seek wisdom and practice humility during the IEP process and notice the difference it makes. The Bible further reiterates that "pride goes before destruction and arrogance before a fall" (Prov. 16:18). As such, we would be wise to avoid arrogance in our teaching and instead practice wisdom and humility. As a Christian educator who is intentional about practicing humility, you have the power to influence people for eternity. What will that look like for you? I want to encourage you to pause and pray now. Ask the Lord what His will is for you as an educator or professional working with students with special needs.

Measurable Annual Goals

Measurable annual goals will be used to determine whether or not the student is making progress throughout the school year and if the IEP is effective for student learning. When annual goals are correctly written in measurable terms, the IEP team will be able to determine whether or not the student is making adequate progress. If it is determined that the student is not making progress, adjustments need to be made to ensure the student's right to a FAPE are not denied. However, if the goals are not written in measurable terms, the IEP team will not know what they are trying to teach and whether or not the student is making progress. What is meant by measurable annual goals?

Measurable Annual Goals:

- Are directly related to the needs identified on the PLAAFP
- Utilize baseline data from the PLAAFP to monitor progress
- Provide a plan for the student's educational goals for the upcoming school year
- Include four components: audience, behavior, criterion, and degree
- Meet the students' needs resulting from the disability that may interfere with the student's progress in the general education curriculum

The measurable annual goals are the big picture of what the student will accomplish this school year and are more global in nature than learning objectives and short-term benchmarks. Writing effective annual goals means that all of the student's deficit areas will be addressed and that the goals will be measurable.

Individuals with Disabilities Education Act (IDEA) requires that the IEP include:

> a statement of measurable annual goals, including academic and functional goals, designed to meet the child's needs that result from the child's disability to enable the child to be involved in and make progress in the general education curriculum; and meet each of the child's other educational needs that result from the child's disability. (IDEA, Section 1414 [d][1][A][i][II])

When writing annual goals, the IEP team must also address all areas of the student's needs which may include academic, functional, social, behavioral, or other areas. One way to ensure that all these needs are met is for the IEP team to refer back to the foundation on which these goals are to be built, the PLAAFP. Again, this is a valid reason why establishing such a solid foundation is critical to student success and to ensuring that a student's FAPE rights are not denied. When referring to the PLAAFP to write the measurable annual goals, the IEP team should consult and consider the information and documentation included such as work samples, standardized assessments, grades, checklists, and information from parents, past teachers, and service providers. Measurable annual goals should be developed using the foundational information on the PLAAFP and supporting documents.

When you are given your first IEP to work with, you will notice that it looks different from the one in this book. The reason is because IEPs vary from school district to school district; IEP forms are not standard in appearance. The same is true for the measurable annual goals section of the IEP. However, the basic components should be the same and the measurable annual goals should include four standard elements as follows:

A. Audience (student)
B. Behavior (observable action)
C. Criterion (measure)
D. Documentation (how it is documented/demonstrated)

Now that you know the four required elements of a measurable annual goal, let us look at an example using Brett's IEP. Brett's sixth measurable annual goal is written as follows:

Annual Goal: Six
Goal: *Speaking/Listening* *In 12 months, Brett will make inferences and draw conclusions in writing and verbally on a written text or other variety of media, read aloud to him as measured biweekly by recorded observations and/or standardized tests with 80% accuracy.*

Every measurable annual goal written should complete the chart below. If all four sections of this chart are not complete, the goal is not precise. You may wonder why it is important to include the audience. One reason for this is to ensure that the goals are written for the student and not for the teacher. It is a common misconception, and error, to write annual goals in terms of what the teacher or service provider will do. Measurable annual goals should always be written in terms of what the student will do.

Audience: *Brett*
Behavior: *will make inferences and draw conclusions in writing and verbally on a written text or other variety of media, read aloud to him*
Criterion: *with 80% accuracy*
Demonstration: *as measured biweekly by recorded observations and/or standardized tests*

Notice that the order of the required elements in this goal are not presented in the exact A, B, C, D order. The order is not an IEP or IDEA requirement, and you will find that these are written in a variety of formats by educators. The important point to remember is to include the four required elements. Another way that this same goal could be written is as follows:

> *Given a written text or other variety of media, read aloud to him, Brett will make inferences and draw conclusions in writing and verbally, as measured biweekly by recorded observations and/or standardized tests with 80% accuracy in 12 months.*

The content is the same; it is just presented in a different order. To further clarify measurable annual goals, let us look at some examples of correctly and incorrectly written goals.

Goal One

Incorrect Goal: *The student will read second grade words aloud to the teacher.*

Audience: *the student*
Behavior: *will read second grade words*
Criterion: missing
Demonstration: missing

Notice that the criterion and demonstration elements are missing. These two elements need to be included for the student to demonstrate the skill and for the teacher to measure the student's progress. Below is the corrected version that contains all four required elements.

Correct Version: *In 36 instructional weeks, the student will read 90 correct words per minute, as measured by second grade DIBELS Next Oral Reading Fluency Passages progress monitoring data.*

Audience: *the student*
Behavior: *will read second grade words*
Criterion: *90 correct words per minute*
Demonstration: *as measured by second grade DIBELS Next Oral Reading Fluency Passages progress monitoring data*

Here is another incorrectly written example:

Goal Two

Incorrect Goal: *The student will demonstrate understanding of a second-grade passage.*

Audience: *the student*
Behavior: missing
Criterion: *a second-grade passage*
Demonstration: missing

Notice that the behavior written is "demonstrate understanding." As stated, this is not an observable behavior. This could have said "demonstrate an understanding by answering comprehension questions," but the way that it is stated it is not observable. Additionally, the demonstration, or how it will be documented, element is missing. Below is the corrected version which contains all four required elements. Again, note that this is not the only way to write this goal, but it is one correctly written version.

Correct Version: *Given a 150-word grade-level 2 reading passage, the student will orally read 100 or more words correctly in 5 min with 90% accuracy in 3/3 consecutive trials by the end of this school year.*

Audience: *the student*
Behavior: *will orally read 100 or more words correctly*
Criterion: *Given a 150-word grade-level 2 reading passage*
Demonstration: *in 5 min with 90% accuracy in 3/3 consecutive trials by the end of this school year*

As you write measurable annual goals for your students, remember that goals and objectives must be directly related to the student's PLAAFP and must include goals and objectives that are both challenging and attainable in 1 year, given the instruction and services the student will receive.

Learning Objectives

Learning objectives differ from measurable annual goals since they are not intended to be global in nature. Whereas the measurable annual goals are intended to state what the student should learn in the upcoming year, the learning objectives lend themselves to attaining the measurable annual goals. **Learning objectives**, sometimes called short-term objectives**,** break down the skills or steps necessary to accomplish a goal into separate components. Learning objectives contain three components as follows:

Learning objectives contain these three components:

1. Behavior—a description of what the student will do
2. Condition—the conditions under which the student will perform the task
3. Criterion—the demonstration for evaluating the performance

Let us look at the learning objectives written for the measurable annual goals above to further distinguish these two concepts.

Annual Goal: Six		
Goal: *Speaking/Listening* *In 12 months, Brett will make inferences and draw conclusions in writing and verbally on a written text or other variety of media, read aloud to him as measured biweekly by recorded observations and/or standardized tests with 80% accuracy.*		
Standard of learning related to this goal: *Virginia Standard 9.2* *The student will produce, analyze, and evaluate auditory, visual, and written media messages.*		
Progress toward this goal will be measured: (Check all that apply)		
___ Tests and Quizzes ___ Standardized Test ___ Norm-Referenced Test ___ Other Assessment	✓ Classwork ___ Projects ___ Homework ✓ Participation	✓ Written Report ✓ Observation ___ Checklist ___ Other
Progress toward this goal will be reported:		
Biweekly		
Short-Term Objectives or Benchmarks, if necessary: or circle if N/A		
Objective/Benchmark One: *Brett will make inferences and draw conclusions based on the text read aloud to him and correctly answer 8 out of 10 questions on a curriculum-based assessment.* Assessment method: *Curriculum-based assessment*		
Objective/Benchmark Two: *Brett will analyze and evaluate a video presentation of a poem delivered via the internet by writing a paragraph drawing accurate conclusions based on the poem as determined by teacher-made rubric with 80% accuracy.* Assessment method: *Teacher graded assignment using rubric*		
Objective/Benchmark Three: Assessment method:		

Notice the two learning objectives are as follows:

Learning Objective One:

Brett will make inferences and draw conclusions based on the text read aloud to him and correctly answer 8 out of 10 questions on a curriculum-based assessment.

1. Behavior—*Brett will make inferences and draw conclusions*
2. Criterion—*correctly answer 8 out of 10 questions on a curriculum-based assessment*
3. Condition—*based on the text read aloud to him*

Learning Objective Two:

Brett will analyze and evaluate a video presentation of a poem delivered via the internet by writing a paragraph drawing accurate conclusions based on the poem as determined by teacher-made rubric with 80% accuracy.

1. Behavior—*Brett will analyze and evaluate a video presentation of a poem delivered via the internet*
2. Criterion—*by writing a paragraph drawing accurate conclusions based on the poem*
3. Condition—*as determined by teacher made rubric with 80% accuracy*

These learning objectives could be completed in one lesson or multiple lessons, but these learning objectives are not a statement of what the student will learn in a year. When writing an IEP make sure that the measurable annual goals and the learning objectives are written with the correct required elements and with the anticipated timeframe in mind.

Benchmarks

Benchmarks are written statements about the major milestones that the student will demonstrate that will lead to the students achieving the measurable annual goals. Benchmarks typically define a given timeframe for a specific outcome or behavior to occur. For example, this could be stated in terms of the school year as "in 36-weeks," or "quarterly." Benchmarks are different from learning objectives because they typically establish increments of achievement that are expected and usually coincide with reporting progress toward the measurable annual goals to parents. Let us look at Brett's IEP to compare his measurable annual goal to the benchmarks that were established for him.

Annual Goal: Five		
Goal: Mathematics In 12 months, when presented with a variety of grade-level multistep linear and quadratic equations, Brett will identify each step and complete them in the correct logical sequential order, as measured weekly by curriculum-based worksheets and assessments.		
Standard of learning related to this goal: Virginia standard A.4 The student will solve multistep linear and quadratic equations with two variables.		
Progress toward this goal will be measured: (Check all that apply)		
✓ Tests and Quizzes ___ Standardized Test ___ Norm-Referenced Test ___ Other Assessment	✓ Classwork ___ Projects ___ Homework ___ Participation	___ Written Report ___ Observation ___ Checklist ___ Other
Progress toward this goal will be reported:		
Biweekly		
Short-Term Objectives or Benchmarks, if necessary: or circle if N/A		
Objective/Benchmark One: In 12 weeks, when presented with 10 multistep linear and quadratic equations for a given variable, Brett will follow the correct logical sequential order to correctly solve the equations with at least 50% accuracy. Assessment method: Curriculum-based worksheets and assessments		
Objective/Benchmark Two: In 24 weeks, when presented with 10 multistep linear and quadratic equations for a given variable, Brett will follow the correct logical sequential order, without teacher support, to correctly solve the equations with at least 80% accuracy. Assessment method: Curriculum-based worksheets and assessments		
Objective/Benchmark Three: Assessment method:		

In most cases, at least two objectives or benchmarks should be written for each annual goal, and progress should be documented on each learning objective or benchmark. Notice that both benchmarks designate a specific timeframe within which Brett is expected to perform specific tasks. He is expected to accomplish 10 multistep equations in 12 weeks with 50% accuracy and then he is expected to accomplish 10 multistep equations with 80% accuracy in 24 weeks without teacher support. These two benchmarks are measurable which will allow the teachers to determine whether or not Brett has made progress toward his measurable annual goal. This information makes it clear and easy to report progress to Brett's parents. If progress is not being made, then another IEP meeting will need to be scheduled. Since measurable annual goals, learning objectives, and benchmarks are required components of the IEP, a meeting must be conducted with all required team members if any of these components are going to be changed. The team will then make the desired changes in the IEP, which will result in a new IEP. There is no such thing as an addendum to an IEP allowed under the current IDEA law (National Association of Special Education Teachers, 2007).

As with all IEPs, differences of opinion will exist, and you may have already determined a more effective way to write the measurable annual goals, learning objectives, or benchmarks for this IEP. That is fantastic. Just as our students are all very unique, educators are unique as well. Every one of us would have approached this student in a different way, and that is okay.

Conclusion

Measurable annual goals serve students by providing a plan for their upcoming school year. This plan is meant to be a roadmap to successful learning based on the student's strengths and needs. Writing measurable annual goals should be a collaborative effort in order to utilize all team member's gifts and talents to promote student learning. When writing measurable annual goals, learning objectives, and benchmarks, it is critical that all required components be included. If changes need to be made, a new IEP will need to be developed. For the Christian educator, prayer and a humble heart should be at the forefront of this endeavor.

Students need a teacher who is patient and willing to help them. Many students with special needs struggle through school. Educators have an opportunity to make a tremendous difference in their lives, and though the IEP process can be overwhelming, teachers who persevere through this process will eventually see positive changes if they do not give up. The Bible says, "Let us not become weary in doing good, for at the proper time we will reap a harvest if we do not give up" (Gal. 6:9).

Chapter Highlights

The Present Levels of Academic Achievement and Functional Performance (PLAAFP) statements are the basis of the goals and services of an IEP.

The PLAAFP serves to inform the IEP team of the student's present abilities, including both strengths and weaknesses.

The purpose of the **measurable annual goals** is to provide a 12-month plan for the student's educational journey.

"Plans fail for lack of counsel, but with many advisers they succeed" (Prov. 15:22).

Ask the Lord what His will is for you as an educator or professional working with students with special needs.

Measurable annual goals will be used to determine whether or not the student is making progress throughout the school year and if the IEP is effective for student learning.

Measurable Annual Goals:

- Are directly related to the needs identified on the PLAAFP
- Utilize baseline data from the PLAAFP to monitor progress
- Provide a plan for the student's educational goals for the upcoming school year
- Include four components: audience, behavior, criterion, degree
- Meet the students' needs resulting from the disability that may interfere with the student's progress in the general education curriculum

IDEA requires that the IEP include:

> a statement of measurable annual goals, including academic and functional goals, designed to meet the child's needs that result from the child's disability to enable the child to be involved in and make progress in the general education curriculum; and meet each of the child's other educational needs that result from the child's disability. (IDEA, Section 1414 [d][1][A][i][II])

When writing annual goals, the IEP team must also address all areas of the student's needs which may include academic, functional, social, behavioral, or other areas.

Learning objectives, sometimes called short-term objectives**,** break down the skills or steps necessary to accomplish a goal into separate components.

Learning objectives contain these three components:

1. Behavior—a description of what the student will do
2. Condition—the conditions under which the student will perform the task
3. Criterion—the demonstration for evaluating the performance

Benchmarks are written statements about the major milestones that the student will demonstrate that will lead to the students achieving the measurable annual goals.

Benchmarks typically define a given timeframe for a specific outcome or behavior to occur.

Benchmarks are different from learning objectives because they typically establish increments of achievement that are expected and usually coincide with reporting progress toward the measurable annual goals to parents.

Chapter Review Questions

1. What is a measurable annual goal, and why are they important? How are they used in the IEP process?
2. Write the four standard elements of measurable goals.
3. Write at least two examples of measurable annual goals.
4. What are learning objectives, and what are the three components of them?
5. Write at least two examples of learning objectives.
6. What are benchmarks?
7. List the differences between measurable annual goals, learning objectives, and benchmarks.

Additional Resources

- For additional information on determining measurable annual goals visit this website: https://www.naset.org/760.0.html
- Here are a couple other sources that you might find useful: https://dpi.wi.gov/sites/default/files/imce/sped/pdf/rda-ccr-iep-measurable-annual-goals-self-check.pdf
- https://www.vbisd.org/cms/lib6/MI01000711/Centricity/Domain/138/Writing%20Measurable%20Annaul%20Goals%20and%20Benchmarks%20-%20Feb%202013.pdf

References

National Association of Special Education Teachers. (2007). Determining measurable annual goals in an IEP. *The Practical Teacher*. Retrieved from: https://www.naset.org/760.0.html

CHAPTER 5

Accommodations, Modifications, Assessments, and Services on the Individualized Education Plan

Learning Outcomes

After reading this chapter, you should be able to:

- ❑ Discuss the biblical perspective that may be applicable to accommodations, modifications, assessments, and services
- ❑ Explain the difference between an accommodation and a modification
- ❑ Name examples of accommodations and modifications and describe how they are different
- ❑ Describe how to determine how a student with disabilities will be assessed
- ❑ Explain the purpose of services for students with special needs
- ❑ Demonstrate an understanding of the role the PLAAFP and the annual goals play in determining service for a student with a disability

Vocabulary

- ❑ Accommodations
- ❑ Modifications
- ❑ Assessments
- ❑ Services
- ❑ Peer-reviewed research

Accommodations, Modifications, Assessments, and Services on an Individualized Education Plan

Writing the Present Levels of Academic Achievement and Functional Performance (PLAAFP) and measurable annual goals on an Individualized Education Plan (IEP) for a student with special needs is no small task. At the opening of the book, you were charged with beginning the IEP process with prayer and encouraged to pray continually throughout the process (I Thess. 5:16–18). At this point, perhaps you have a better understanding of why prayer is such an integral part of the IEP process for the Christian educator. We need the wisdom and strength of the Lord to accomplish the task before us. One verse I value is Colossians 1:11, which says, "We also pray that you will be strengthened with all his glorious power so you will have all the endurance and patience you need. May you be filled with joy." Not only does this verse offer us hope that the Lord will be with us throughout the process, but it encourages us to be filled with joy as we strive to accomplish this task. I love the thought of teachers finding joy in serving others just as Christ came to serve us.

Another verse that I find myself reading serves as a reminder to choose wisely as I consider all of the possible accommodations, modifications, assessments, and service options for students with disabilities. Let us consider Leviticus 19:14 which states, "You shall not curse a deaf man, nor place a stumbling block before the blind, but you shall revere your God; I am the LORD" (Amplified Bible). This verse speaks directly to us as we contemplate how to provide a quality education for our students. Certainly, the straightest road with the fewest speedbumps is the quickest to travel, but it is not always the most scenic or gratifying. The purpose of the IEP is not simply to make the students life easier. If that were the case, we would just eliminate all challenging assignments. There is a much greater purpose for accommodations, modifications, assessments, and services than making the students life easier. Let us take a closer look at each one.

Accommodations

According to the law, the IEP must contain a statement of any individual accommodations that are necessary to measure a student's progress based on the information in the student's PLAAFP. Providing accommodations as part of the instructional and assessment process should allow the student equal opportunity to access the curriculum and give the student a chance to demonstrate progress. Accommodations will also provide access to nonacademic and extracurricular activities and educationally related settings, which are also required by law. We noted the importance of not putting a stumbling block in the way of our students which could keep them from making educational progress. It is also important to note that it is not appropriate to provide accommodations or modifications based on enhancing a student's performance beyond providing equal access.

Accommodations and modifications may seem very similar; however, the impact that each has on the student's education is different. An **accommodation** changes HOW a student learns. For example, students in the general education classroom may be assigned to write a five-page book report after reading a classic novel. A student with a specific learning disability may be accommodated to allow this student to listen to an audio version of the classic novel instead of reading it. The student would then complete the same five-page book report as other students in the general education classroom. This changes how the student learned the information.

An

Accommodation

changes

HOW

a student learns

Below is a list of more examples of HOW a student may be accommodated. This is certainly not an exhaustive list, but each accommodation is one that students with disabilities may need, depending on their unique situation.

Accommodations

- Provide a quiet testing atmosphere
- Test in a small-group setting
- Provide extended time within the same day
- Administer the test in smaller sections, but within the specified time constraint
- Abridge directions for easier understanding
- Using Braille or large print books for students with a vision disability
- Present in sign language for deaf/hard of hearing students
- Provide sign language interpreters
- Read and provide directions in the student's native language
- Provide breaks during instruction
- Instructions and/or content read aloud, as appropriate
- Allowing the student to sit on an exercise ball instead of a chair
- Moving obstacles so students in wheelchairs have better access and mobility
- Weighted vests
- Providing notes for the student
- Providing audio books instead of requiring them to read the print books

The accommodations in the list above are all examples of how students learn. As we look at accommodations and modifications, remember that specific detailed information added on the PLAAFP serves as the foundation for these decisions. The data from the PLAAFP may be used to justify or support recommendations for special education or related services, testing, accommodations, and modifications (Patti, 2016).

Modifications

Though accommodations may lessen the effects of a student's disability on grade-level curriculum and assessments, they are not intended to reduce the learning expectations. In contrast, modifications may change, lower, or reduce the learning expectations (Cortiella, 2005). **Modifications** change WHAT a student learns.

A

Modification

changes

WHAT

A student learns

Below is a list of examples of WHAT may be modified for the student based on his or her individual disability.

Modifications

- Reduced number of test items
- Allowing outlining instead of a book report, essay, or project
- Grammar and spellcheck support

- Modified workload or length of assignments/tests
- Parts of the test read aloud to the student
- Allow use of a calculator or manipulatives (when not given to other students)
- Provide extra text to promote understanding
- Teacher assistance by pointing or providing written cues on the test (such as a "STOP" indicator).

As stated above, modifications change WHAT a student learns. In the example of the student above, the students in the general education classroom were assigned to write a five-page book report after reading a classic novel. The student with a specific learning disability was accommodated by allowing him to listen to an audio version of the classic novel instead of reading it. The student was then required to complete the same five-page book report as students in the general education classroom. If we were to offer a modification for this student, we might allow the student to write an outline of the novel that he listened to instead of writing a five-page book report. This modifies what was expected of the student.

Accommodations and Modifications for Brett

Now let us look at Brett's IEP again to learn more about accommodations and modifications. I want to reiterate that this example is not the perfect IEP, but as a Christian educator, we must try our best to determine the needs of the student, and then decide how we will meet those needs. Providing accommodations and modifications is one way that we can help meet the student's needs. We are to do the best we can with the knowledge we have and apply it to each unique student so as to meet his or her unique needs. Read the Accommodations/ Modifications on Brett's IEP below.

Liberty Academic School

Individualized Education Plan
Least Restrictive Environment
Accommodations/Modifications

Student Name: Brett Smith Meeting Date: 9/20/21

This student will be provided access to the general education, special education, other school services and activities, and education-related settings:

______ With no accommodations/modifications

__✓__ With accommodations/modifications as follows:

Accommodations/Modifications					
Accommodations/ Modifications	Delivery Recommendations	Least Restrictive Environment	Frequency	Duration	Services Begin
Tests and assignments read aloud to student	As needed	Special education classroom	Daily	During instructional class time or during tests	9/23/22
Support for organizational skills	Agenda checked daily by teacher at end of class	Special and general education classroom	Conclusion of every class	Throughout the school day	9/23/22
Refocusing and redirection	Brett requires assistance in attending to classroom activities	Special and general education classroom	Daily	Throughout the school day	9/23/22
Strategic Seating	Brett focuses best when placed in close proximity to the teacher near the front of the room	Special and general education classroom			9/23/22
Copy of class notes	As needed	Special and general education classroom			9/23/22
Extended time for assessments	As needed	Special and general education classroom	As needed	During assessments	9/23/22

Notice this list of accommodations provided for Brett. The list includes accommodations for HOW he will learn, and it does not include modifications regarding WHAT he will learn.

Accommodations
Tests and assignments read aloud to student
Support for organizational skills
Refocusing and redirection
Strategic seating
Copy of class notes
Additional time on assessments

When you are in a situation that requires accommodations and modifications, remember to ask yourself, "Does this change HOW the student is learning?" If so, it is an accommodation. If not, ask yourself, "Does this change WHAT the student is learning?" If so, it is a modification. Hopefully, this makes these two concepts easier to differentiate. Now that we have a better understanding of accommodations and modifications, let us look at assessments.

Assessments

Assessments are one form of measuring a student's progress toward meeting the annual goals on the students' IEP. Students with disabilities participate in the general education state and district-wide assessments to the greatest degree possible, which requires the IEP team and teachers to monitor the student's progress because students with special needs will be assessed just as their nondisabled counterparts (National Center for Educational Outcomes, 2003). Students with disabilities taking the same state and district-wide assessment as their general education peers will do so on the same schedule as those without disabilities. This means that all students will participate in the federally mandated testing timelines for specific grades and subjects, but just as checking with your specific state is important to know which assessments are offered, it is also important to check with your state to see how often students are required to be assessed and which assessments are required at the state level. As a general rule, if the students in the general education classroom are being assessed, the students with special needs should be assessed as well.

When an IEP team determines that a student requires modifications to the state or district-wide assessments, it is essential that the alternate means be valid and reliable in order to determine student progress.

Each state and district has specific approved alternate assessments which an IEP team may choose to require the student with a disability to take instead of the one used by the general education students. Once again, the IEP team needs to be familiar with these state and district requirements in order to abide by legal obligations.

If the IEP team provides accommodations (changing HOW the assessment is given), this does not fundamentally alter the assessment. However, if the IEP team provides modifications, (changing WHAT is assessed), this does fundamentally alter the assessment.

If the student requires accommodations or modifications for instruction or assessment in the general education curriculum or classroom, the IEP team needs to consider this when deciding on how to measure student progress. If the student receives accommodations or modifications in the classroom, it is likely that the student will need those same accommodations and modifications for state and district-wide assessments. However, this may not always be the case, depending on the subject being assessed.

If the IEP team determines that the student is not able to participate in all or part of the state or district-wide assessments, even with accommodations provided, the IEP team must select an alternate assessment for the student. This is another instance where it is important for you, as an IEP team participant, to be aware of your specific state's offerings. Not all states offer all assessment options. To best meet the needs of the students with disabilities, it is essential that the IEP team members be aware of the assessment options offered in their state. Let us look at Brett's IEP for further clarification.

Liberty Academic School

Individualized Education Plan
Assessments

Individual testing accommodations, specific to the student's disability and needs, to be used consistently by the student in the recommended educational program and in the administration of district-wide assessments of the student achievement and, in accordance with department policy, state assessments of student achievement as indicated below.

______ No testing accommodations are recommended OR

Testing Accommodation	Condition	Implementation Recommendations
Describe the type, length, and purpose of the test upon which the use of testing accommodations is conditioned, if applicable. Identify the amount of extended time, type of setting, etc., specific to testing accommodations, if applicable.		
• Time and a half extended time • Administered in special education classroom • Use of a computer	For all quizzes/tests: Read aloud to student Use of computer	Tests administered in a small group (3-5 students) Computer used to read to the student and/or to type answers

Narrative Explanation of Assessment Decision
Due to Brett's specific learning disability, he is given extended time on assignments and tests. He is easily distracted and thus will benefit from being away from distractions and allowed to complete assignments and tests with a small group of students or in a one-on-one setting. The use of computer aides with specially designed instruction such as web-based instructions and the use of earphones, will be allowed.

Participation in State and District-wide Assessments

__✓__ The student will participate in the same state and district-wide assessments administered to the general education students.

______ The student will participate in an alternate assessment on a state or district-wide assessment of student achievement. If checked, identify the alternate assessment below.

____
Alternate Assessment

Note the reason the student will not participate in the same state and district-wide assessments administered to the general education students and why the specific alternative assessment is appropriate.

Notice that Brett will receive extended time on his tests, the test will be administered in a separate classroom, he will be allowed to use a computer, and the information on the quizzes and tests may be read aloud to him. All of these alter HOW he will be assessed and not WHAT he will be assessed. They are all accommodations, not modifications. Because Brett's PLAAFP does not indicate that he meets the criteria for an alternative assessment, and he is not receiving modifications, the IEP should indicate that he will participate in the same assessments as the general education students.

Services

Determining services for students can be easy for some students, as the need is obvious, such as when a student in a wheelchair is in need of transportation. Other services may be much more elusive and challenging to determine and provide.

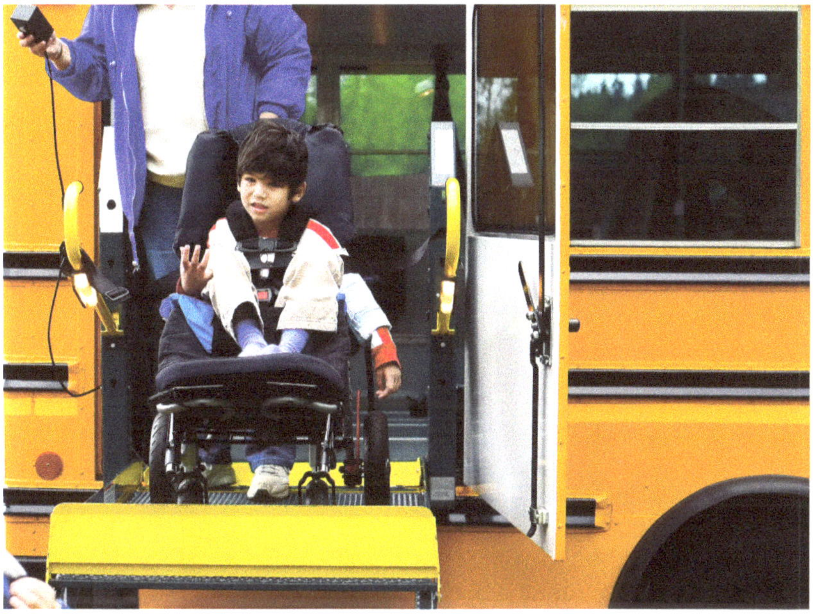

© Jaren Jai Wicklund/Shutterstock.com

> IDEA requires that IEPs include a statement of the special education and related services and supplementary aids and services, based on peer-reviewed research to the extent practicable, to be provided to the child, or on behalf of the child, and a statement of the program modifications or supports for school personnel that will be provided for the child (20 U.S.C. § 1414 [d][1][A][i][IV]).

The **services** portion of the IEP is meant to explain how the school will help the student achieve his or her annual goals and make progress in the general education curriculum. This requires that the teacher utilize the information on the students PLAAFP in combination with the annual goals to determine what, if any, services should be provided for the student.

As indicated before, it is important that these services be determined on an individual basis. There is no "one-size-fits-all" education, and this certainly holds true for the services portion of the IEP. The IEP team should consider the students present abilities and challenges, in combination with the measurable annual goals determined for the student, and decide which services need to be provided to ensure that the student is able to reach the designated measurable annual goals.

For the services, educators should identify the service(s), including frequency, duration, and instructional setting that will be provided for the student to receive a free appropriate public education. Services described must be provided as scheduled except when the school is closed or on partial days. Additionally, special education services and supplementary aids should be based on peer-reviewed research. **Peer-reviewed research** refers to research vetted by qualified reviewers (i.e., through a peer review process) to ensure that the quality of the information meets the standards of the field before the research is published (Yell, Katsiyannis, Ennis, Losinski, & Christle, 2016).

Here are a few examples of services that may be provided for students with special needs:

Services

- Speech-language pathology services
- Audiology services
- Transportation
- Medical services
- Occupational therapy
- Physical therapy
- Psychological services
- Recreation
- Counseling services
- School health services
- Social work services in schools
- Orientation and mobility services
- Special education

Now let us look at Brett's IEP to see what services he will receive.

Liberty Academic School

Individual Education Program
Related Services

	Related Services					
Service	Service Delivery Recommendations	Person Responsible	Instructional Setting	Frequency	Duration	Services Begin
Speech/ Language Therapy	Small group (5:1)	Mr. Greer	Therapy room	Twice weekly	40 mins	Beginning 10/19/22

~ Identify, if applicable, class size, language (if other than English), group or individual services, direct and/or indirect consultant teacher services, or other service delivery recommendations.

12-Month Service and/or Program

Student is eligible to receive special education services and/or program during July/August:

Yes or **No** (circle one)

If yes,

__✓__ Student will receive the same special education program/services as recommended above.

OR

______ Student will receive the following special education program/services:

Special Education Program/Services	Service Delivery Recommendations	Instructional Setting	Frequency	Duration	Services Begin

Based on Brett's PLAAFP and the annual goals written on his IEP, it was determined that he needed speech/language therapy. What information may have been used to determine that Brett needed this service?

In reviewing Brett's PLAAFP and annual goals, we see the following information, which led to this decision:

This information is located in the PLAFFP section of his IEP under Summary of Academic Achievement:

Reading/Written Language

Speech and language reevaluation reveals a Core Language score (76 SS) in the borderline range; however, significant improvement is noted from previous test score (61SS). During his twice-weekly 30-min speech/language therapy sessions, Brett exhibits effort on a mostly consistent basis. The speech/language pathologist noted improvements in verbal comprehension based on test scores 73 (SS) and improved participation based on teacher observation. Brett continues to work on soliciting additional info or asking for repetition when unsure.

Reading comprehension skills (94 SS) and decoding skills (93 SS) are in the average range. He can decode and answer basic comprehension questions. Long-term retention of material is an area of concern. Word reading (75 SS) is in the borderline range. Significant deficits are noted in listening comprehension (60 SS). Effort was inconsistent during testing. For example, Brett asked random off-topic questions and was redirected by the teacher twice. Additionally, shortly after Brett began reading the third section of the reading comprehension section, he put his head down on the desk to take a break twice.

Test Results:

WIAT—III (01/12/2020)
Basic Reading 84 (Standard Score), 14 (Percentile Rank)
Essay Comp: Grammar & Mechanics 82 (SS), 10 (PR)
Essay Composition 77 (SS), 5 (PR)
Expressive Vocabulary 74 (SS), 4 (PR)
Listening Comprehension 60 (SS), 0.3 (PR)
Oral Discourse Comprehension 56 (SS), 0.2 (PR)
Oral Expression 87 (SS), 19 (PR)

Oral Language 70 (SS), 2 (PR)
Oral Reading Accuracy 75 (SS), 5 (PR)
Oral Reading Fluency 82 (SS), 13 (PR)
Oral Reading Rate 84 (SS), 14 (PR)
Oral Word Fluency 96 (SS), 38 (PR)
Reading Comprehension 93 (SS), 32 (PR)
Receptive Vocabulary 92 (SS), 3 (PR)
Sentence Building 74 (SS), 4 (PR)
Sentence Combining 84 (SS), 14 (PR)
Sentence Composition 78 (SS), 7 (PR)
Sentence Repetition 100 (SS), 50 (PR)
Spelling 80 (SS), 9 (PR)
Theme Development and Text Organization 67 (SS), 1 (PR)
Total Achievement 71 (SS), 3 (PR)
Total Reading 82 (SS), 12 (PR)
Word Count 89 (SS), 23 (PR)

Word Reading 75 (SS), 5 (PR)
Written Expression 74 (SS), 4 (PR)
Wechsler Abbreviated Scale of Intelligence-II
Full Scale IQ 73 (SS), 5 (PR)
Perceptual Reasoning 78 (SS), 7 (PR)
Verbal Comprehension 73 (SS), 4 (PR)

CELF-5
Core Language Score 76 (SS), 5 (PR)
Formulated Sentences 6 (SS), 9 (PR)
Recalling Sentences 8 (SS), 25 (PR)
Semantic Relationships 5 (SS), 5 (PR)
Understanding Spoken Paragraphs 5 (SS), 5 (PR)

Speech/Language:

Brett is a considerate, respectful, and typically engaged student. His attention issues present a challenge quite often, but he responds when redirected. Brett is able to participate in conversational dialogue, but he is negatively impacted by language processing and auditory memory problems. He frequently demonstrates difficulty with higher-order questions and organizing sentences when incorporating abstract ideas, but is able to use basic communication skills. Brett has been working on strategies to improve his word retrieval and auditory memory skills, but he continues to struggle. Brett's articulation is characterized by a distortion of the /p/ phoneme in many positions of words and blends.

Speech/Language:

Brett needs to develop language processing, verbal/written expression, auditory memory, and word retrieval skills. Therapist support is needed in order to monitor his articulation of the /p/ phoneme in structured speech and spontaneous conversation.

Summary:

Brett has a significant delay in written expression, language skills, speech skills, attention skills, math calculation, and math concepts, which interferes with age-appropriate activities in the general education curriculum.

This seems a bit like detective work, but as the student's educator and advocate, this is what is needed and expected. Could there be more information in the PLAAFP that would help make the determination to offer Brett speech/language therapy? Certainly. Is this more than enough information? To some educators, yes. To others, perhaps not. To a large degree, this is a subjective task, which is why it is so important that the PLAAFP be completed with a substantial amount of significant information. These services may be critical for a student's education. Without a strongly built PLAAFP, it may be hard to justify providing the help that the student so aptly needs.

Is there information in Brett's annual goals that may have helped to determine that he needs speech/language therapy? There should be. Below are two of his annual goals that are directly related to speech/language therapy.

Annual Goal: Seven		
Goal: Speech/Language In 12-months, Brett will monitor and produce the /p/ phoneme in all positions of words and in conversational speech, as measured biweekly by recorded observations and/or tests, with 80% accuracy.		
Standard of learning related to this goal: Virginia Standard 9.1d 9.1d) Use grammatically correct language, including vocabulary appropriate to the topic, audience, and purpose.		
Progress toward this goal will be measured: (Check all that apply)		
✓ Tests and Quizzes ___ Standardized Test ___ Norm Referenced Test ___ Other Assessment	✓ Classwork ___ Projects ___ Homework ✓ Participation	___ Written Report ✓ Observation ___ Checklist ___ Other
Progress toward this goal will be reported:		
Bi-weekly		
Short-Term Objectives or Benchmarks, if necessary: or circle if N/A		
Objective/Benchmark One: Given a topic, Brett will produce grammatically correct language, including the /p/ phoneme, in a written short story with 80% accuracy. He will monitor and self-correct the paper. The final version will be submitted to fulfill the 80% accuracy requirement. Assessment method: Self-monitoring/correcting and teacher-graded submission		
Objective/Benchmark Two: Given a topic, Brett will produce grammatically correct language, including the /p/ phoneme, in a short story, as presented aloud to the teacher, with 80% accuracy, as determined by participation and teacher observation. Assessment method: Participation and teacher observation		
Objective/Benchmark Three: Assessment method:		

Annual Goal: Eight		
Goal: Speech/Language In 12-months, Brett will use retrieval strategies, as measured biweekly by recorded observations and/or standardized tests, with 80% accuracy.		
Standard of learning related to this goal: Virginia standard 9.1f and 9.1h f) Use verbal and nonverbal techniques for presentation. h) Give impromptu responses to questions about presentations.		
Progress toward this goal will be measured: (Check all that apply)		
___ Tests and Quizzes _X_ Standardized Test ___ Norm Referenced Test ___ Other Assessment	___ Classwork ___ Projects ___ Homework ___ Participation	___ Written Report _X_ Observation ___ Checklist ___ Other
Progress toward this goal will be reported:		
Biweekly		
Short Term Objectives or Benchmarks, if necessary: or circle if N/A		
Objective/Benchmark One: After a classroom presentation, Brett will answer orally delivered content questions related to the presentation, as given by the teacher. He will use retrieval strategies to answer the questions with 80% accuracy as determined by teacher observation. Assessment method: Teacher observation		
Objective/Benchmark Two: Given a standardized test, Brett will score 80% accuracy in the language sections requiring retrieval strategies as determined by standardized test and teacher observation. Assessment method: Standardized test and teacher observation		
Objective/Benchmark Three: Assessment method:		

Notice that two of his annual goals are specifically related to speech/language:

1. *In 12 months, Brett will monitor and produce the /p/ phoneme in all positions of words and in conversational speech, as measured biweekly by recorded observations and/or tests, with 80% accuracy.*
2. *In 12 months, Brett will use retrieval strategies, as measured biweekly by recorded observations and/or standardized tests, with 80% accuracy.*

These two annual goals may be addressed with speech/language therapy. Students need to make progress toward their annual goals. Providing this service for Brett will help him to achieve these two annual goals. Progress toward his annual goals will be measured via a standardized test and biweekly throughout the year, when Brett is expected to average 80% or higher by observations recorded by the person in charge of his speech/language therapy. Did you notice that on the "Excusal Notice" Russ Greer asked to be excused from the meeting? He is the speech/language therapist. In this situation, Mr. Greer is having surgery on the day of the IEP meeting. How would you choose to handle this? The meeting could be moved to an earlier or later date, or the meeting could continue without him. This is the type of situation that IEP team members will encounter, and decisions will need to be made that are in the best interest of the child.

Conclusion

Accommodations, modification, assessments, and services are all exceptionally important elements of the IEP. Since completing these tasks requires perseverance and wisdom, it is essential that we seek the Lord throughout this process. Accommodations change *How* a student learns while a modification changes *What* a student learns. Assessments should be given in regular intervals and at least as often as students in the regular education classroom. Services should be determined based on the PLAAFP and the measurable annual goals.

Romans 14:13 says, "Therefore let us not pass judgment on one another any longer, but rather decide never to put a stumbling block or hindrance in the way of a brother" (English Standard Version). The message here can be applied to the entire IEP process. Unless the whole child is considered, including the student's disability, these decisions could become a stumbling block and a hindrance to the student's success. By understanding the significance of the choices we make, educators can offer accommodations, modifications, assessments, and services to further the academic achievement and functional success of their students.

Chapter Highlights

According to the law, the IEP must contain a statement of any individual accommodations that are necessary to measure a student's progress based on the information in the student's PLAAFP.

Providing accommodations as part of the instructional and assessment process should allow the student equal opportunity to access the curriculum and give the student a chance to demonstrate progress.

Accommodations and modifications may seem very similar; however, the impact that each has on the student's education is different.

An **accommodation** changes HOW a student learns.

Though accommodations may lessen the effects of a student's disability on grade-level curriculum and assessments, they are not intended to reduce the learning expectations.

Modifications change WHAT a student learns.

Assessments are one form of measuring a student's progress toward meeting the annual goals on the students' IEP.

Students with disabilities participate in the general education state and district-wide assessments to the greatest degree possible, which requires the IEP team and teachers to monitor the student's progress because students with special needs will be assessed just as their nondisabled counterparts (National Center for Educational Outcomes, 2003).

As a general rule, if the students in the general education classroom are being assessed, the students with special needs should be assessed as well.

If the IEP team provides accommodations (changing HOW the assessment is given), this does not fundamentally alter the assessment. However, if the IEP team provides modifications, (changing WHAT is assessed), this does fundamentally alter the assessment.

The **services** portion of the IEP is meant to explain how the school will help the student achieve his or her annual goals and make progress in the general education curriculum.

For the services, educators should identify the service(s), including frequency, duration, and instructional setting that will be provided for the student to receive a free appropriate public education.

Peer-reviewed research refers to research vetted by qualified reviewers (i.e., through a peer review process) to ensure that the quality of the information meets the standards of the field before the research is published (Yell, Katsiyannis, Ennis, Losinski, & Christle, 2016).

Chapter Review Questions

1. Locate another verse from the Bible that could be applied to accommodations, modifications, assessments, and services, and elaborate on how this verse could be applicable.
2. Describe the importance of having appropriate accommodations, modifications, assessments, and services for students with disabilities or special needs.
3. What are the differences between accommodations and modifications?
4. List three accommodations not indicated in the chapter.
5. List three modifications not listed in the chapter.
6. How does a teacher decide which assessment(s) a student with disabilities is qualified to take?
7. Under what circumstances should students be offered services, and how are they determined?
8. List three services not discussed in the chapter.

Additional Resources

- For additional information on services visit this website: http://www.doe.virginia.gov/special_ed/iep_instruct_svcs/stds-based_iep/training_modules/module_5_identifying_special_ed_related_services.pptx
- For additional information on supports visit this website: http://www.projectgenesis.us/services/sess/
- For additional information on IEPs visit this website: https://www2.ed.gov/parents/needs/speced/iepguide/index.html

References

Cortiella, C. (2005). No Child Left Behind: Determining appropriate assessment accommodations for students with disabilities. *National Center for Learning Disabilities.* Retrieved from http://www.ldonline.org/article/10938

Individuals with Disabilities Education Act. 20 U.S.C., §§ 1400, et seq.

National Center for Educational Outcomes. (2003). *Accountability for assessment results in the No Child Left Behind Act: What it means for children with disabilities.* Minneapolis, MN: University of Minnesota.

Patti, A. L. (2016). Back to basics: Practical tips for IEP writing. *Intervention in School and Clinic*, *51*(3), 151–156. doi:10.1177/1053451215585805

Yell, M. L., Katsiyannis, A., Ennis, R. P., Losinski, M., & Christle, C. A. (2016). Avoiding substantive errors in individualized education program development. *Teaching Exceptional Children*, *49*(1), 31–40. doi:10.1177/0040059916662204

CHAPTER 6

Least Restrictive Environment

Learning Outcomes

After reading this chapter, you should be able to:

- ❑ Define Least Restrictive Environment (LRE)
- ❑ Address misconceptions about LRE
- ❑ Identify how LRE is addressed in an IEP
- ❑ Describe possible biblical implications of choosing the LRE
- ❑ Describe the balance between LRE and FAPE

Vocabulary

- ❑ Least Restrictive Environment (LRE)
- ❑ Learning Environment

Least Restrictive Environment

Prior to 1975, public schools were not required to educate any child with a disability, but with the passage of the Education of All Handicapped Children Act (EAHCA) in 1975, public schools were required to provide all students with a disability a free appropriate public education (FAPE). Although early special education laws mentioned educating students with disabilities alongside their nondisabled peers, it took years for this concept to develop into what is now known as the Least Restrictive Environment or LRE. Current Individuals with Disabilities Education Act (IDEA) law requires that a student with a disability be educated in the LRE and defines this requirement as follows:

> To the maximum extent appropriate, children with disabilities, including children in public or private institutions or other care facilities, are educated with children who are not disabled, and special classes, separate schooling, or other removal of children with disabilities from the regular educational environment occurs only when the nature or severity of the disability of a child is such that education in regular classes with the use of supplementary aids and services cannot be achieved satisfactorily (IDEA, 20 U.S.C. § 1412 [612][a][5][A]).

This portion of the law can sometimes cause confusion. While the goal throughout the Individualized Education Plan (IEP) process is to identify appropriate special education services and placement for a student, it can appear that the intent of this section of the law is intended to minimize services. This, however, is not the case. This chapter will address what LRE means and how this concept might impact the development of an IEP.

© wavebreakmedia/Shutterstock.com

Clarification of the LRE

It is a common misconception in special education that more is better. Educators, and even parents, may have the purist intentions when they try to include additional services in an IEP to provide a student with as much support as possible to help them be successful in the classroom. However, the goal of an IEP, and special education in general, should be to provide the appropriate amount of support to allow the student to function, to the best of his or her ability, without support. This is one of the best ways to prepare the student for life following high school graduation. To clarify what that means, we need to look at the purpose of public education, as a whole.

Students typically attend school for 12 to 14 years prior to graduating from high school. During that time, much of the focus is on short-term success such as understanding the current lesson or topic and making good grades. Even long-term goals are usually focused on promotion to the next grade-level or eventual graduation, but those goals are just the beginning. The ultimate goal of a public education is to prepare a student to be a successful adult. For some this means entering the work force and living independently, while for others it may mean several more years of formal education. There are many options for a student when he or she graduates from high school; hopefully, an appropriate education will prepare the student to successfully take the next step into adulthood.

For a student who receives special education services, the long-term goal is the same or similar: to prepare for the next phase of life. With that in mind, the focus of an IEP should not just be to help the student to succeed in school, but to prepare the student to be a successful adult. Although these goals may seem to be similar, they can sometimes be contradictory when determining special education services. For instance, while providing a student with more services might be helpful in the classroom, providing fewer services may help the student become more independent. When writing an IEP, it is important to attempt to meet the academic and emotional needs of the student, while also being cognoscente of what services the student can do without. Trying to provide every possible service may seem like the most supportive and caring approach, but it may sometimes be a hindrance to the student's ability to function independently, which would likely be an unintentional stumbling block. Remember Leviticus 19:14 says, "You shall not curse a deaf man nor place a stumbling block before the blind, but you shall revere your God; I am the Lord" (Amplified Bible). Providing an excess of services may actually hinder the student from learning to function independently.

While providing more services might help a student in the classroom, providing fewer services may help the student become more independent.

In addition to academic performance, the social and emotional needs of the student need to be considered. For example, a student may be able to make better grades in a self-contained special education classroom, but his or her social skills may be more likely to develop in a general classroom setting; both aspects should be considered when determining the LRE for the student.

Environment Defined

In order to address the LRE in an IEP, it is important to first identify what is included in an environment. The word environment often brings to mind physical surroundings, and this is, in fact, an important aspect of the LRE. However, it is important to look at the big picture when considering the learning environment for a student who receives special education services. The **learning environment** is the physical location where the student is receiving his or her education. All elements of the IEP must be considered when making this decision. The law states that, to the "maximum extent appropriate," a student with a disability should be educated with students who are not disabled. The law also uses the term "regular classes" to describe the standard for which placement is to be compared.

To carry this concept a step further, educating a student with a disability in a regular classroom suggests that the intent is for the student to participate in that "regular" class to the maximum extent appropriate. Therefore, the intent of placing a student who has a disability in a regular classroom according to the **LRE** is not just to place him or her physically in the same location, but to provide comparable instruction and social interaction. The law also addresses "supplementary aids and services" as a means to provide support and instructional differentiation. If a student is capable of participating in regular classroom activities, to isolate the student in the back of the room and provided separate instruction would not be meeting the intent of the LRE, even though the student would physically be in the regular classroom. To the greatest degree possible, the student with a disability should participate in the same manner that students in the regular classroom are participating.

What Is "Least Restrictive"

When describing the LRE, the word "Restrictive" is not used in a common fashion. In an IEP, the word restrictive actually refers to the services and setting (environment) provided. The word restrictive describes the degree in which special education services hinder a student from receiving instruction in a regular classroom setting. In other words, when a student receives special education services, he or she may be "restricted" from receiving regular educational services. Therefore, a student receiving special education services should be placed in an environment as close to a regular classroom as possible.

As stated earlier in the book, special education teachers must work with regular classroom teachers, as well as other educators, to provide a quality education for students with a disability. When choosing the most appropriate LRE for a student, this decision should be based exclusively on the needs of the student and not on the desire of teachers to work together or to avoid working together. A Christian educator's goal should be to help students work through their burdens and not add to them (Ackerman, 2012). This typically requires that teachers work together to support the student with his or her disability. The Bible says, "Bear one another's burdens, and so fulfill the law of Christ" (Gal. 6:2, English Standard Version). This goes back to building quality relationships and working together. Classrooms cannot function effectively as learning environments unless harmonious relationships exist (Van Brummelen, 2009).

Practically speaking, what does LRE placement look like? Although the law specifically identifies the importance of educating a student with a disability alongside nondisabled students, there are other settings that could also be considered restrictive. Placing a student into an environment other than the school they would attend if they did not have a disability, or placing a student in a different age-group are examples of other restrictions that should be considered. "School districts are required by law to offer a continuum of alternative placements so that teams have the opportunity to review educational contexts from least restrictive to more restrictive for each student in special education" (McCloskey, 2016, p. 1204). Again, the focus must be kept on meeting the needs of the student.

Figure 6.1 identifies levels of special education services and which services might be considered most to least restrictive:

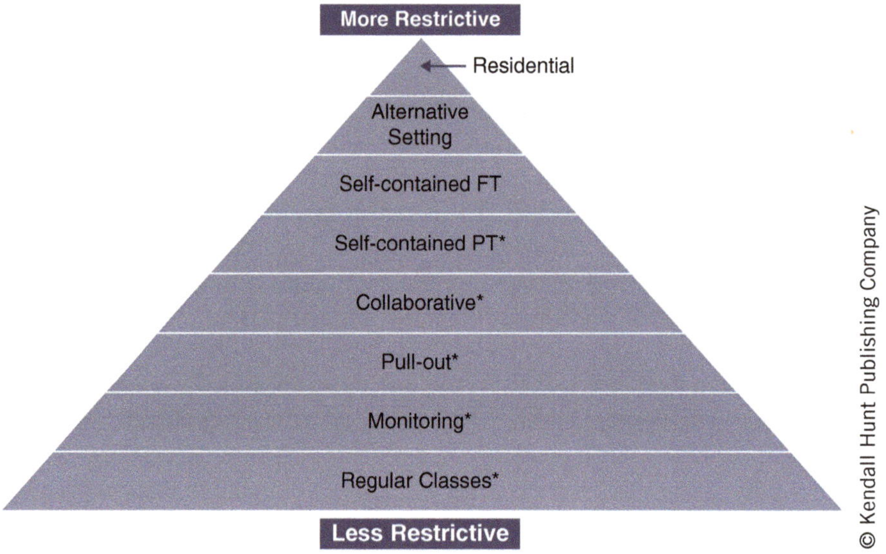

Figure 6.1. Pyramid showing possible levels of restrictive environments or special education services. *Services include at least some instruction in a regular classroom setting.

In reviewing Figure 6.1, keep in mind that terms describing the level of special education services may vary between states, districts, and even schools, and this is not an exhaustive list, but most public schools provide many, if not all, of these types of services. The descriptions of the levels of service, beginning with the bottom of the triangle (least restrictive) and going to the top (most restrictive), are as follows:

- Regular Classes—Student is placed in a regular classroom with his or her peers and receives no special education services.

- Monitoring—Student has an IEP but receives few or no services in class. Student may occasionally or regularly meet with a special education representative and/or academic and social progress may be reviewed regularly.
- Pull-out—Student is in a regular classroom the majority of the time but is occasionally taken out of the regular classroom setting for separate individual or group instruction or counseling.
- Collaborative—Student is placed in a regular classroom setting but receives support from a special education teacher in the regular classroom. The special education teacher works collaboratively with the regular education teacher and may serve one student, or several students with disabilities.
- Self-contained Part Time—Student is placed in a regular or collaborative classroom for some instruction but also receives some instruction in a separate special education environment.
- Self-contained Full Time—Student is in a separate special education setting for most or all of his or her instruction. Instruction is provided by one or more special education teachers.
- Alternative Setting—Student is served in a nontraditional setting, often in a separate location from the traditional school.
- Residential—Student receives short-term or long-term services in the home, usually by a special education teacher or specialist.

FAPE Versus Least Restrictive Environment

IDEA law requires that all children have access to and receive a free appropriate public education or FAPE. The definition of "appropriate" is determined through the IEP process based on the needs of the individual student receiving special education services. FAPE does not mean that a student must receive all available resources; it only means that the IEP should address the individual needs of the student in a reasonable manner to promote academic progress. Academic progress cannot, and should not, be defined the same for every student.

One challenge often faced in developing an effective IEP is identifying an environment that balances the need for sufficient (appropriate) resources, while keeping the student in the LRE. In other words, how does the IEP meet the needs of the student while not providing an unnecessarily restrictive environment? If it is possible to meet the needs of a student with resources and supplementary aids in a regular classroom, that is strongly preferred over taking the student out of the regular classroom, even for comparable services. Inversely, if a student cannot be successful in a regular classroom due to the severity of his or her disability, it is the school's obligation to place the student in a more restrictive environment (Kauffman & Hallahan, 2011).

LRE in the IEP

Identifying the LRE is an important part of the IEP process. Deciding on the appropriate environment can be challenging but often becomes clearer over time, and with increased familiarity with the student. Reviewing the student's prior placement, current available settings, and feedback from all members of the IEP team can help guide the process. However, the LRE should be reviewed regularly and changed to be either more or less restrictive when and if it is appropriate. Identifying the LRE is not always a progression toward a more restrictive or less restrictive environment. A student who was not successful in a regular classroom setting in middle school, may mature enough to find success in a less restrictive high school setting. Contrariwise, a student may face greater challenges, and need a more supportive environment, as he or she grows older. At times, it may even be necessary to experiment with a new setting to determine how the student will respond.

Conclusion

Although many of the terms used to identify the LRE can be subjective (i.e., adequate, appropriate, satisfactorily), it is best to take a big picture approach and ask the right questions. Striving to place a student in a setting that provides the needed resources, while also allowing the student to receive instruction in a general education classroom to the greatest degree possible, can increase the student's opportunity for success in the classroom and beyond.

Chapter Highlights

The Least Restrictive Environment is:

> To the maximum extent appropriate, children with disabilities, including children in public or private institutions or other care facilities, are educated with children who are not disabled, and special classes, separate schooling, or other removal of children with disabilities from the regular educational environment occurs only when the nature or severity of the disability of a child is such that education in regular classes with the use of supplementary aids and services cannot be achieved satisfactorily (IDEA, 20 U.S.C. § 1412 [612][a][5][A]).

The goal of an IEP, and special education in general, should be to provide the appropriate amount of support to allow the student to function, to the best of his or her ability, without support.

The ultimate goal of a public education is to prepare a student to be a successful adult.

While providing a student with more services might be helpful in the classroom, providing fewer services may help the student become more independent.

Providing an excess of services may actually hinder the student from learning to function independently.

The **learning environment** is the physical location where the student is receiving his or her education.

The law states that, to the "maximum extent appropriate," a student with a disability should be educated with students who are not disabled.

The intent of placing a student who has a disability in a regular classroom according to the **LRE** is not just to place him or her physically in the same location, but to provide comparable instruction and social interaction.

Classrooms cannot function effectively as learning environments unless harmonious relationships exist (Van Brummelen, 2009).

IDEA law requires that all children have access to and receive a free appropriate public education or FAPE.

Chapter Review Questions

1. What is the overall goal or purpose of the LRE portion of IDEA law?
2. What are the practical implications of the LRE in the development of an IEP?
3. Identify three additional Bible verses that educators could refer to when making the decision about the LRE in terms of building relationships.
4. How can a balance of sufficient services and a less restrictive environment be achieved?
5. What information should be considered when identifying the LRE for a student?
6. Identify the progression of services from least to most restrictive.

Additional Resources

- To review case law regarding LRE visit this website and navigate to Chapter 9: https://books.google.com/books?hl=en&lr=&id=XjJZBwAAQBAJ&oi=fnd&pg=PA107&dq=least+restrictive+environment&ots=7wWV4QvIxq&sig=K_fHQcRqh9JGSEgzQ0G2VBC6Euw#v=onepage&q=least%20restrictive%20environment&f=false
- To read the portion of IDEA law that includes reference to LRE visit this website: http://uscode.house.gov/view.xhtml?path=/prelim@title20/chapter33&edition=prelim
- To read a letter from the U.S. Department of Education regarding preschool LRE visit this website: https://www2.ed.gov/policy/speced/guid/idea/memosdcltrs/preschoollre22912.pdf

References

Ackerman, B. (2012). *G.U.I.D.E. Differentiated instruction for Christian educators.* Lynchburg, VA: Liberty University Press.

Individuals with Disabilities Education Improvement Act of 2004. 20 U.S.C, §§ 1400, et seq.

Kauffman, J. M., & Hallahan, D. P. (Eds.). (2011). *Handbook of special education.* New York, NY: Routledge.

McCloskey, E. (2016). To the maximum extend appropriate: Determining success and the least restrictive environment for a student with autism spectrum disorder. *International Journal of Inclusive Education, 20*(11), 1204–1222. doi:10.1080.13603116.2016.1155667

Van Brummelen, H. (2009). *Walking with God in the classroom: Christian approaches to teaching and learning* (3rd ed.). Colorado Springs, CO: Purposeful Design Publications.

CHAPTER 7

The Transition Plan

Learning Outcomes

After reading this chapter, you should be able to:

- ❑ Describe the importance of having a biblical perspective and how it applies to the transition process
- ❑ Summarize the purpose of the transition plan and what is required to be included in a transition plan
- ❑ Define and give examples of transition assessments
- ❑ Identify the four major transition goals
- ❑ Explain the importance of the transition plan and which students need to have a transition plan
- ❑ Compare the sections of a transition plan and describe what belongs in each

Vocabulary

- ❑ Transition plan
- ❑ Transition assessment
- ❑ Post-secondary goal
- ❑ Jobs and employment goal
- ❑ Vocational training goal
- ❑ Independent living goal

The Transition Plan

The purpose of the **transition plan** for students with disabilities is to help them achieve their post-high-school goals, such as attending college or having a career. The guiding principles of the transition plan are addressed in the Individuals with Disabilities Education Act (IDEA) and the Rehabilitation Act of 1973 (Rehabilitation Act). These statutes document the requirements of a transition plan and emphasize that this plan should be a collaborative effort with specific attainable transition goals clearly stated. Services to achieve these goals must also be provided, and progress must be monitored to ensure students meet their goals. The transition plan is meant to provide a detailed path for successfully transitioning the high school student into the adult world beyond high school.

© Syda Productions/ Shutterstock.com

To aspire to leadership is an honorable ambition.
1 Timothy 3:1

As an educator, you have the opportunity to influence future generations. Throughout your teaching career, you could easily impact thousands of people with your leadership. To aspire to leadership is an honorable ambition (1 Tim. 3:1) and teachers are typically seen as leaders, but not all leaders are perceived or judged to the same degree. The Bible says "Not many of you should become teachers, my fellow believers, because you know that we who teach will be judged more strictly" (James 3:1). I find this verse motivating because the Individualized Education Plan (IEP) process is long and detailed, and it requires dedication and perseverance. Understanding that I am held to a higher standard encourages me to continue to seek the Lord daily and to rely on Him to provide all that I need to successfully serve my students. "True greatness, true leadership, is found in giving yourself in service to others, not in coaxing or inducing others to serve you. True service is never without cost" (Sanders, 1994, p. 15). Jesus is the ultimate example of sacrificial leadership. He came to serve, and not to be served. As you traverse the IEP process, reflect on the type of leader you desire to be. Leaders are needed who are authoritative, spiritual, and sacrificial. Authoritative leaders are needed because people want leaders who know where they are going and know how to get there. Spiritual leaders are needed because, without a strong relationship with the Lord, even the most competent person cannot lead people to Christ. Sacrificial leaders are needed because this follows the model of Jesus, Who gave Himself for the whole world and Who calls us to be like Him (Sanders, 1994). What kind of leader will you be? Being intentional about your leadership will help you to achieve your goal.

Let Them Dream

The law requires that students with disabilities who are 16 years of age (or earlier if deemed necessary) must have a transition plan. Many students who are 14 to 18-years old are still unaware of the skills they possess that would serve them as an adult intending to get a college education or take advantage of a career opportunity. Many are still trying to determine their likes and dislikes and their strengths and weaknesses. This is a time in a student's life when a teacher can have an extremely positive or negative impact on the outcomes for his or her life. Students need encouragement. You may have a student communicate that he or she wants to become a doctor or lawyer or other challenging profession, and you may feel certain that this student will never be able to accomplish this. How will you respond without crushing his or her spirit and self-esteem, understanding that the goals you choose must be attainable and must be of interest to the student? This is not an easy decision to make.

© AnemStyle/Shutterstock.com

Let me encourage you with the story of Temple Grandin. She did not speak her first word until she was 3 ½ years old. After years of struggling, she was diagnosed with autism. Today, she is a well-respected Professor of Animal Science at Colorado State University and the designer of livestock handling facilities in the United States, Canada, Europe, Mexico, Australia, New Zealand, and other countries. She has starred in multiple movies, authored many books, and is a world renowned motivational speaker. She oftentimes speaks of the difference her teachers made in her life. The influence educators have is powerful and may be used to encourage students with disabilities to achieve abundantly more than many people may believe that they are able to. Students with special needs and their families need teachers who believe in them and will offer them hope and encouragement. As a Christian educator, how will you address the transition plan for your students? How will you encourage them? Your answers to these questions will be life-changing for the students entrusted to you.

Transition Plan

Transition planning is a mandated component of IEPs that is designed to ensure a successful transition to adult life for students with disabilities. How do we get students from dreaming to achieving? We design their coursework and educational experiences to help them achieve the transition goals set for them. This is a plan to help each student achieve his or her post-high-school goals. The planning process must begin for a student no later than when the student turns 16 (earlier, if deemed necessary). In some states, the transition plan process begins at age 14.

© vectorfusionart/Shutterstock.com

Transition Assessment

A **transition assessment** may be given to provide information necessary to develop transition goals. These assessments or surveys are designed to examine and reveal student preferences, interests, strengths, and personality traits. The results are used, along with student input, to write the transition goals. Rating scales and questionnaires that assess student's job readiness in terms of employability skills, such as social skills and daily living skills are quick ways to gather student, parent, and teacher input on the student's readiness for a job. This information may then be used to provide activities and services to further meet the student's needs so as to accomplish his or her transition goals. The results of these assessments should serve as the basis for the transition goals. IDEA mandates that student preferences and interests be considered when developing the transition plan and that his or her plans after high school should guide his or her course of study and transition services.

Transition Goals

The transition plan must contain appropriate measurable goals based on age-appropriate transition assessments related to four major areas including post-secondary education, employment/jobs, vocational training, and independent living.

1. Post-Secondary Education
2. Jobs and Employment
3. Vocational Training
4. Independent Living

The **post-secondary goal** is intended to support the student in furthering his or her post-secondary education goals such as attending a college or university. The **jobs and employment goal** is intended to identify the occupation the student desires to do after graduation. The **vocational training goal** is meant to ensure that the student has the proper education and experience to learn a trade. The **independent living goal** serves to identify the student's needs for independent living skills and to provide the needed supports and services to achieve these goals. All four of these should guide the decisions regarding services in high school.

This part of the IEP must be individualized, just as all other components. The assessment should be used to help determine these goals, but it is also helpful to know the student and to include the student in the conversation. The IEP team leader should also solicit information from the student's parents and prior year's teacher.

Transition goals must be reviewed and updated annually, along with the rest of the IEP. Since some transition plans may start as early as age 14, some students may be in middle school when this process beings. Transition goals for these students may be more general in nature. For example, the transition goal for a middle school student may indicate the desire to work with cars. However, as the student gets older, the goal may become more specific and he or she could indicate the desire to become an auto mechanic. The students' goal may change multiple times over the years, which is typically reflective of growth and maturity. When students graduate or leave high school, they receive a Summary of Performance. This document contains information regarding the student's academic achievement and functional skills. It also offers recommendations for achieving postsecondary goals.

Transition Services

Services for a student with special needs is one way of assisting the student with meeting his or her goals. Oftentimes, services are confused with accommodations and modifications. Remember that accommodations change *how* the student learns, and modifications change *what* a student learns. Services are related to post-high-school activities to support the student in achieving his or her post-high-school goals. The U.S. Department of Education (2017) defines transition services as follows:

TRANSITION SERVICES

> Transition Services means a coordinated set of activities for a student with a disability designed within a results-oriented process that is focused on improving the academic and functional achievement of the child with a disability to facilitate the child's movement from school to post-school activities, including postsecondary education, vocational education, integrated employment (including supported employment), continuing and adult education, adult services, independent living, or community participation. The coordinated set of activities is based on each student's needs, taking into account the student's strengths, preferences, and interests, and includes instruction, related services, community experiences, the development of employment and other post-school adult living objectives, and, if appropriate, the acquisition of daily living skills and provision of a functional vocational evaluation. (20 U.S.C. § 1401[34])

In many cases, because they are not equipped to do so, the school is not able to provide all of the services requisite for students with special needs. This means that schools will need to invite outside organizations to participate in the IEP process, and representatives need to attend IEP meetings. Examples of such outside organizations are employment agencies, local businesses, counseling services and/or organizations, companies that have job related training (on-the-job training), college admissions counselors, vocational rehabilitation offices, group homes, organizations that provide independent living training, organizations, and programs that teach self-advocacy skills, work study programs, and so on.

Based on the student's transition goals, the IEP team needs to decide what services are necessary to help the student meet his or her needs. These may include:

- Instruction (including special education)
- Related Services (such as speech/language therapy)
- College and Career Counseling
- Community Experiences (internship/volunteer)
- Daily Living Skills Training

After the IEP team has decided which services the student needs, accommodations may be listed as well. IEP goals may also be used to support the transition plan. For example, if the student wants to attend auto mechanic school, he or she may need to learn specific science or math skills. As a result, the team may need to write IEP goals and provide school services to teach related science and math skills. Not all transition services occur in the school. Some may take place in the home or in the community. This is also true for transition goals related to independent living skills.

Independent Living Skills

For the student with disabilities who desires to live independently after high school, acquiring independent living skills is a necessity. This process must be individual and intentional. Some examples of independent living skills are listed below.

- Using public transportation
- Purchasing and maintaining a car (including securing auto insurance)
- Opening and manage a bank account
- Scheduling and attending medical appointments
- Shopping for groceries and preparing meals

Independent living skills are a critical component of the transition process. These skills need to be addressed and assessed in a way so that the student and family achieve their desired result for the student's adult life.

Brett's Transition Plan

Now let's look at Brett's Transition Plan. Notice there are two documents below:

1. A cover page for quick reference, and
2. The transition plan that offers more detail.

Cover Page

The cover page states the student's contact information, disability, parents' names, important dates, and participants involved. This allows the reader to view pertinent information quickly. The dates of the transition plan meeting should coordinate with the IEP meeting since both of these plans need to be reviewed annually. Having both on the same day and same time will also help ensure that the IEP team members are present for the transition plan meeting.

Liberty Academic School
XXXX XXXX XXXXXX
XXXXXXX XXXXXX
XXXXXXX XXXXXX
Telephone: XXXXXX
Fax: XXXXXXXXXX
Email: xxxxx@xxxx.com
Website: www.xxxxxxx.com

Individualized Education Plan
Transition Plan Cover Page

Student Name: Brett Smith Date: 9/6/22

Disability: Intellectual Disability

Grade: 9th DOB: 3/24/07 Age: 15

Parent/Guardian Name: David & Mary Smith

Street Address: 1101 First Street

City: Majestic State: VA Zip Code: 12345

Phone #: 123-456-7890

A copy of the IEP was given to the parent/guardian/student on: 9/7/18

IEP Team Leader: Kelly Garman Phone #: 111-111-1111

The Individualized Education Plan (IEP) that accompanies this document is meant to support the team approach to ensuring successful outcomes for the student. The IEP is a working document that outlines the student's strengths, needs, and vision for the future. The intent of an IEP is to bring together a team of people who understand and support the student in order to come to a consensus on a transition plan that is appropriate and effective for the student.

Important Details to Document	Date
Transition IEP will be reviewed no later than	7/19/22
Parent notified of Transition Plan IEP Meeting	9/6/22
Student notified of Transition Plan IEP Meeting (if applicable)	N/A
Transition Plan IEP Meeting	9/20/22
Most recent eligibility date	2/15/22
Next Re-evaluation, including eligibility, must occur before	7/19/24

Participants Involved

The list below indicates that the individual participated in the development of the IEP and the decisions regarding placement. Participation does not authorize consent. Parent consent (or student if 18+) is indicated on the "Prior Notice" page.

Name of Participant	Position
David & Mary Smith	Father and Mother
Brett Smith	Student
Shonda Miller	Administrator
Kelly Garman	Special Education Teacher, Team Leader
Stuart Fisher	General Education Teacher
Dr. Nathaniel Salinas	Guidance Counselor
Russ Greer	Speech-language Therapist

Individualized Education Plan
Transition Cover Page, continued

The parent and student must be notified at least one year prior to the student turning 18 that the IDEA procedural safeguards will transfer to the student at the age of 18. This notice must be accompanied by an explanation of those procedural safeguards. If applicable, sign below documenting notification.

Parent Signature: ______________________________

Student Signature: ______________________________

Date informed: ________9/20/22________________

IEP Team Member or Administrator Signature: ____Kelly Garman______

Diploma and Transition Status

Projected Graduation Date: May, 2026

Is the student projected to graduate/exit this school year? Yes or (No) (circle one)
If yes, inform the parents and student that a *Summary of Performance* will be provided prior to graduating/exiting school.

Will the student be graduating with a standard, technical, or higher-level diploma or exceeding the age of eligibility this year? Yes or (No) (circle one)
If yes, a *Summary of Performance* must be provided to the student prior to graduating or exceeding the age of eligibility.

This student is a candidate for:	
______ Advanced Studies Diploma	______ Modified Standard Diploma
______ Advanced Technical Diploma	______ Special Diploma
__✓__ Standard Diploma	______ Certificate of Completion Program
______ Technical Diploma	______ General Education Diploma
______ General Achievement Diploma	______ Not discussed at this time

The second page of the Transition Cover Page contains information about the procedural safeguards for the student and parent(s). This notification is a lawful requirement, as the student and parent(s) must be notified at least 1 year prior to the student turning 18 that the procedural rights will transfer from the parent(s) to the student. This page also includes the diploma and transition status. Notice that the IEP team anticipates that Brett will graduate with a standard diploma. All of his goals should reflect this choice. For example, he should not have goals that fundamentally alter the curriculum since doing so would indicate that he would graduate with a modified diploma.

Liberty Academic School
XXXX XXXX XXXXXX
XXXXXXX XXXXXX
XXXXXXX XXXXXX
Telephone: XXXXXX
Fax: XXXXXXXXXX
Email: xxxxx@xxxx.com
Website: www.xxxxxxx.com

Individualized Education Plan
Transition Plan

Transition plans should begin no later than when the student is 16 years of age, or earlier if required by state law or if deemed necessary by the IEP team. The plan for transition services must be discussed and documented annually.

Student Name: Brett Smith Age: 14

Date Form Completed: ______________________

Anticipated Graduation Date: May, 2026

Current IEP Dates from: 9/20/22 to: 9/20/23

Post-Secondary Goal

In the box below, write the student's post-secondary goal. This goal should be written in collaboration with the IEP team including the family and student. Include preferences, interests, and desired outcomes for post-secondary education, training, employment, and adult living.

Brett's goal is to attend vocational training and earn his certification as an auto-mechanic. He wishes to work at his neighbor's auto repair shop as a mechanic. He intends to live independently.

In the box below, write the disability-related skills that require IEP goals and/or related services. Consider all disability-related skills necessary for the student to achieve the stated post-secondary vision noted above.

In consideration of the present levels of performance, transition service needs of the student focus on the student's courses of study, taking into account the student's strengths, preferences, and interests as they relate to transition from school to post-school activities. Brett needs to further develop work-related skills and self-advocacy skills. He will complete the necessary coursework required for graduation with a Liberty Academic High School standard diploma. He needs to develop skills that will allow him to live independently, however, these skills are taught in the 10th and 11th grade curriculum.

Individualized Education Plan
Transition Plan, continued

Transition Plan Activities		
Needed Activities to Facilitate the Student's Movement from School to Post-School Activities	**Service/Activity**	**School/District/Agency Responsible**
Instruction	~ Review high school course syllabi for class preferences, with a focus on courses/ electives in auto mechanics ~ Participate in general education elective courses and notify teachers of accommodations/ modifications ~ Participate in IEP meetings and communicate personal accommodations, assist in the development of goals, and articulate personal modifications needed in an educational setting ~ Manage time schedules for daily and long-term assignments/projects	~ Student, parent, guidance counselor ~ Student, general education teacher, special education teacher ~ Student, parent, general education teacher, special education teacher, guidance counselor, psychologist ~ Student, special education teacher
Related Services	Speech/Language Therapy to improve communication skills	~ Student, Speech/ Language Therapist
Community Experiences	Participate in community service activities/internship through auto mechanics course	~ Student, general education teacher
Development of Employment and other Post-High School Adult Living Objectives	Create a profile on Career Zone to research and further refine career preferences in auto mechanics	~ Student, special education teacher, guidance counselor
Daily Living Skills (if applicable)	Considering Brett's current levels of performance, Daily Living Skills (DLS) is not needed at this time	N/A
Functional Vocational Assessment (if applicable)	Considering Brett's current levels of performance, Functional Vocational Assessment (FVA) is not needed at this time	N/A

Transition Plan

Notice that Brett's transition plan clearly states his transition goal, which is:

> *Brett's goal is to attend vocational training and earn his certification as an auto mechanic. He wishes to work at his neighbor's auto repair shop as a mechanic. He intends to live independently.*

Even at the age of 14, he has a clear idea of what he wants to do and where he wants to do it. He wants to be an auto mechanic, and he wants to do so at his neighbor's repair shop. It would not suffice for the IEP team to simply write "to obtain employment" for Brett's transition goal, as this does not give the team a clear direction for Brett's desire to become an auto mechanic. Remember that the Transition Plan goals must be specific and measurable if they are to help Brett achieve his post-high-school goal of becoming an auto mechanic. He also plans to live independently. Since Brett is only 14, his plan could easily change over time, but for now, your goal as an educator is to support this plan. Now we need to consider all disability-related skills necessary for the student to achieve his goal. This is what was considered:

> *In consideration of the present levels of performance, transition service needs of the student focus on the student's courses of study, taking into account the student's strengths, preferences, and interests as they relate to transition from school to post-school activities. Brett needs to further develop work-related skills and self-advocacy skills. He will complete the necessary coursework required for graduation with a Liberty Academic High School standard diploma. He needs to develop skills that will allow him to live independently, however, these skills are taught in the 10th and 11th grade curriculum.*

Notice that essentially all of the information on Brett's IEP was considered in this decision. Once again, the Present Level of Academic Achievement and Functional Performance (PLAAFP) is shown to be foundational and the goals critical to ensure that Brett's educational needs are met. The transition plan provides the guidance necessary for Brett to reach his transition goal. Now let's look at the activities needed to direct his instruction.

Included in his plan are very specific elements related to his instruction. Notice that some of the activities are to be completed collaboratively by the student and teacher(s), such as "Review high school course syllabi for class preferences, with a focus on courses/electives in auto mechanics" and "Manage time schedules for daily and long-term assignments/projects." Others are the responsibility of multiple team members such as "Participate in general education elective courses and notify teacher of accommodations/modifications" and "Participate in IEP meetings and communicate personal accommodations, assist in the development of goals, and articulate personal modifications needed in an educational setting." It is always important to note the responsible parties to ensure that someone addresses each activity.

Speech/Language Therapy is indicated as a transition service. This will help Brett to achieve his goal since communication skills are critical to employment. Also, he will gain insightful experience through his community service activities, which are part of the curriculum requirements in his auto mechanics course. His guidance counselor and special education teacher plan to work with him to create a profile in Career Zone to help him refine in career preferences. All of these activities and services are skillfully designed to help Brett achieve his ultimate post-high-school goal of being an auto mechanic in his neighbor's auto repair shop.

Conclusion

When you are writing a transition plan, I want to encourage you to dream big for your students. Ask their opinions and take the steps necessary to help them achieve their goals. Remember that you may be their only hope of getting to do what they want as a career. I encourage you not to hinder them but to support and encourage their desires as much as possible, while making sure the goals are attainable. Remember that the verse, "I can do all things through Christ who gives me strength" (Phil. 4:13) applies to the student with a disability just as it applies to everyone else.

Chapter Highlights

The purpose of the **transition plan** for students with disabilities is to help them achieve their post-high-school goals, such as attending college or having a career.

The transition plan is meant to provide a detailed path for successfully transitioning the high school student into the adult world beyond high school.

"True greatness, true leadership, is found in giving yourself in service to others, not in coaxing or inducing others to serve you. True service is never without cost" (Sanders, 1994, p. 15).

Jesus is the ultimate example of sacrificial leadership. He came to serve, and not to be served.

The law requires that students with disabilities who are 16 years of age (or earlier if deemed necessary) must have a transition plan.

Students need encouragement.

The influence educators have is powerful and may be used to encourage students with disabilities to achieve abundantly more than many people may believe that they are able to.

Students with special needs and their families need teachers who believe in them and will offer them hope and encouragement.

Transition planning is a mandated component of IEPs that is designed to ensure a successful transition to adult life for students with disabilities.

A **transition assessment** may be given to provide information necessary to develop transition goals.

IDEA mandates that student preferences and interests be considered when developing the transition plan and that his or her plans after high school should guide his or her course of study and transition services.

The transition plan must contain appropriate measurable goals based on age-appropriate transition assessments related to four major areas including post-secondary education, employment/jobs, vocational training, and independent living.

The **post-secondary goal** is intended to support the student in furthering his or her post-secondary education goals such as attending a college or university.

The **jobs and employment goal** is intended to identify the occupation the student desires to do after graduation.

The **vocational training goal** is meant to ensure that the student has the proper education and experience to learn a trade.

The **independent living goal** serves to identify the student's needs for independent living skills and to provide the needed supports and services to achieve these goals.

Transition goals must be reviewed and updated annually, along with the rest of the IEP.

Services for a student with special needs is one way of assisting the student with meeting his or her goals.

Services are related to post-high-school activities to support the student in achieving his or her post-high-school goals.

TRANSITION SERVICES

> Transition Services means a coordinated set of activities for a student with a disability designed within a results-oriented process that is focused on improving the academic and functional achievement of the child with a disability to facilitate the child's movement from school to post-school activities, including postsecondary education, vocational education, integrated employment (including supported employment), continuing and adult education, adult services, independent living, or community participation. The coordinated set of activities is based on each student's needs, taking into account the student's strengths, preferences and interests, and includes instruction, related services, community experiences, the development of employment and other post-school adult living objectives, and, if appropriate, the acquisition of daily living skills and provision of a functional vocational evaluation. (20 U.S.C. § 1401[34])

Not all transition services occur in the school. Some may take place in the home or in the community.

Chapter Review Questions

1. Why is it important to have a biblical perspective when working with students during the transition process? Identify at least two Scripture passages to support your stance.
2. What is the purpose of the transition plan?
3. What needs to be included in all transition plans? What else can be included in a transition plan?
4. Define transition assessment. Write at least four examples of transition assessments.
5. How many major transition goals are there? List those goals.
6. At what age are students required to have a transition plan? How often do transition plans need to be written/revised, and through what age?
7. Why are transition plans important?
8. What are the major sections of a transition plan? Give examples of what would be included, in each section.

Additional Resources

- To see a Transition Guide to Post-secondary Education and Employment for Students and Youth with Disabilities, visit this website: www2.ed.gov/about/offices/list/osers/transition/products/postsecondary-transition-guide-2017.pdf
- To learn more about Dr. Temple Grandin, visit this website: http://grandin.com/

References

Individuals with Disabilities Education Act of 2004. 20 U.S.C., §§ 1400, et seq.

Sanders, J. O. (1994). *Spiritual leadership: Principles of excellence for every believer*. Chicago, IL: Moody Press.

U.S. Department of Education, Office of Special Education and Rehabilitative Services. (2017). *A transition guide to postsecondary education and employment for students and youth with disabilities*, Washington, D.C. Retrieved from: www2.ed.gov/about/offices/list/osers/transition/products/postsecondary-transition-guide-2017.pdf

CHAPTER 8

Implementing an Individualized Education Plan

Learning Outcomes

After reading this chapter, you should be able to:

- ❑ Summarize the steps involved in implementing an IEP
- ❑ Describe the elements of the IEP
- ❑ Explain action items as they relate to the IEP
- ❑ Write a measurable outcome and goal that could be included in an IEP appropriate for a student with special needs

Vocabulary

- ❑ Action Items

Implementing an Individualized Education Plan

Now that the Individualized Education Plan (IEP) has been written, how should an educator work toward successfully implementing it? Throughout this process, you have taken a team approach to working with the student this school year. Hopefully, you have presented yourself with godly character in all your ways. This begins with the initial contact with the student, to meeting the family, to soliciting the help of all team members, and to conducting the IEP meeting. The Bible says in James 3:13, "Who is wise and understanding among you? Let them show it by their good life, by deeds done in the humility that comes from wisdom." You have worked hard and made many decisions regarding a student's roadmap to his or her education for the upcoming year. Now that it is time to implement the IEP, there are several lawful requirements that educators must be aware of when implementing an IEP. For example, Individuals with Disabilities Education Act (IDEA) regulations require that "as soon as possible following development of the IEP, special education and related services are made available to the child in accordance with the child's IEP" (34 C.F.R. §300.323[c]). This means that as soon as the IEP is written, and without unnecessary delay, the students IEP goals and services should be implemented. Additionally, the student's IEP must be readily available to each teacher, related services provider, or any other service provider responsible for its implementation (34 C.F.R. §300.323[d][1]). It is a best practice to provide a copy of the IEP to all responsible parties and to document the receipt of the information by each recipient.

> *"Who is wise and understanding among you? Let them show it by their good life."*
> *James 3:13*

Looking back at the IEP, remember that each element of the IEP contains action items. Action items require someone to take action to get the item accomplished. According to IDEA,

> Schools must ensure that every staff person responsible for implementing the IEP is "informed of his or her specific responsibilities related to implementing the child's IEP; and the specific accommodations, modifications, or supports that must be provided for the child in accordance with the IEP." (34 C.F.R. §300.323[d][2])

Let's revisit the main elements of the IEP to get a closer look at what the implementation process may look like and how to indicate the party or parties responsible for each item.

Prior to implementing the IEP, the team leader must present the parents/guardians with Prior Notice and Parental Consent form to sign. The form for Brett's parents to sign is below.

Liberty Academic School
XXXX XXXX XXXXXX
XXXXXXX XXXXXX
XXXXXXX XXXXXX
Telephone: XXXXXX
Fax: XXXXXXXXXX
Email: xxxxx@xxxx.com
Website: www.xxxxxxx.com

Individualized Education Plan
Prior Notice and Parental Consent

Student Name: Brett Smith

Meeting Details:

IEP Meeting Date: 9/20/22

Meeting Time: 1:30

Meeting Location: D221

Please complete and return this form to:

Kelly Garman	Kgarman@email.com	(111)-111-1111
Team Leader	Email	Phone Number

This document serves as notice prior to implementing this IEP. The decisions made in this IEP are based on a review of the students Present Levels of Academic and Functional Achievement. Relevant documentation to these decisions, if any, are attached. If you need additional information or have concerns, please contact the team leader.

Parent/Adult Student Consent: Indicate your decision by checking the appropriate space below and sign.

__✓__ I GIVE permission to implement this IEP.

______ I DO NOT GIVE permission to implement this IEP.

David Smith
Parent or Adult Student Signature

9/20/22
Date

Transfer of Rights at the Age of Majority (age 18)

Indicate the date that the student and parent were informed of the transfer of parental rights under IDEA to the adult student at the age of 18. This must occur at least one year prior to the student turning 18 years of age.

I was informed of the parental rights under IDEA and that these rights transfer to me at age 18.

____
Adult Student Signature

____
Date

I was informed of the parental rights under IDEA that transfer to my child at age 18.

____
Parent Signature

____
Date

Once the appropriate signatures have been secured and the document has been added to the official IEP, it is time to begin the implementation process. Though there are several approaches that could be utilized, the approach that I prefer is to revisit each of the major sections of the IEP to determine actions items. I define **action items** as anything on the IEP that someone needs to do to help the student accomplish his or her goals and to receive services. A specific person should be assigned to each action item to guarantee that each item is accomplished. Let us revisit the IEP to determine our action items and the person(s) responsible for ensuring that the items get accomplished. The major sections we will revisit include:

Present Level of Academic Achievement and Functional Performance (PLAAFP)
Measurable Annual Goals
Accommodations/Modifications
Related Services
Least Restrictive Environment (LRE)
Assessments
Transition Plan

Since the PLAAFP is the foundational document, it is a good idea to begin with this document.

Present Level of Academic Achievement and Functional Performance

On the PLAAFP, there are not any specific action items to complete at this point in the IEP process. The PLAAFP should still be taken into consideration throughout the implementation process because this is the baseline measurement indicating where the student began his or her educational journey for this school year. At the end of the school year, the team should be able to look at the PLAAFP and see the progress that the student made based on where he or she began. The reason the IEP was written with observable and measurable goals so that educational growth be documented, and to some degree quantified.

Measurable Annual Goals

Let us look at the Measurable Annual Goals page to determine the action items that require attention. In many situations, implementing these goals will require multiple people and will usually include the special education teacher and the general education teacher, though it could also include specialists. The subject of Brett's first annual goal is reading and has several components that need to be implemented including:

- The measurable annual goal
- How the progress will be measured
- How the progress will be reported
- Short-term benchmarks/objectives
- Assessments

Here is what his first Measurable Annual Goal looks like:

Annual Goal: One		
Goal: *Reading* *In 12 months, Brett will read and exhibit comprehension of the ninth grade text, including prose, drama, poetry, and content area subject text in 80% of given opportunities, as measured biweekly on teacher-devised tests or text worksheets.*		
Standard of learning related to this goal: *Virginia Standard 9.4* *The student will read, comprehend, and analyze a variety of literacy texts including narratives, narrative nonfiction, poetry, and drama.*		
Progress toward this goal will be measured: (Check all that apply)		
✓ Tests and Quizzes ___ Standardized Test ___ Norm Referenced Test ___ Other Assessment	✓ Classwork ___ Projects ___ Homework ✓ Participation	___ Written Report ✓ Observation ___ Checklist ___ Other
Progress toward this goal will be reported:		
Biweekly		
Short-Term Objectives or Benchmarks, if necessary: or circle if N/A		
Objective/Benchmark One: *Given a literacy text, Brett will read aloud and explain the author's main idea and purpose in a writing sample, based on a rubric, in three out of four trials by December 13, 2022.* Assessment method: *Teacher observation and writing rubric*		
Objective/Benchmark Two: *Given a literary text, Brett will define the relationships between and among elements of literature: characters, plot, setting, tone, point of view, and theme in three out of four trails by March 13, 2023.* Assessment method: *Writing elements rubric*		
Objective/Benchmark Three: *Given a literary text, Brett will analyze how an author's specific word choices and syntax achieve special effects and support the author's purpose. The literary text will be read, and Brett will correctly answer 80% of the questions pertaining to the text in three out of four trials as graded by end-of-novel test.* Assessment method: *End of novel test*		

Though there is not usually a place directly on the annual goals section of the IEP to note who is responsible for each component, I find that it is helpful for clarity and accountability to write who is responsible for each action item beside each goal. This information is oftentimes found on the Accommodations/Modification page. For example, for the above components, the name of each person could be written directly next to each action item as indicated in the sections below.

The Measurable Annual Goal

Since Brett's first goal is in reading, and it states that, "*In 12 months, Brett will read and exhibit comprehension of the ninth grade text, including prose, drama, poetry, and content area subject text in 80% of given opportunities, as measured biweekly on teacher-devised tests or text worksheets,*" he may need have this goal assigned to the general education teacher and the special education teacher since he may be able to read some of the assignments himself in the general education classroom, but "as needed," he may go to the special education classroom to have his assignments and/or tests read to him by the special education teacher. The chart below is located on the Accommodations page of his IEP.

Accommodations/Modifications					
Accommodations/ Modifications	Delivery Recommendations	Least Restrictive Environment	Frequency	Duration	Services Begin
Tests and assignments read aloud to student	*As needed*	*Special education classroom*	*Daily*	*During instructional class time or during tests*	*9/23/22*

How Student Progress Will Be Measured?

The special education teacher is ultimately responsible for this goal and is also responsible for measuring and documenting progress toward this goal. As noted on the Measurable Annual Goals above, and seen below, this progress will be measured in four ways: tests and quizzes, classwork, participation, and observation.

Progress toward this goal will be measured: (Check all that apply)		
✓ Tests and Quizzes	✓ Classwork	___ Written Report
___ Standardized Test	___ Projects	✓ Observation
___ Norm Referenced Test	___ Homework	___ Checklist
___ Other Assessment	✓ Participation	___ Other

What happens if the special education teacher would like to measure this goal by having the student complete a project, but this was not initially indicated on the IEP? Does the special education teacher have the freedom to add a checkmark to "projects" in this section? Absolutely! There will be many, many times throughout the IEP implementation process that changes may need to occur. It is the IEP team's responsibility to ensure that all the components of the IEP are met, which means that deleting items from the IEP would, in most cases, require parental and IEP team approval, but in a situation like this, it is fine to add a project for Brett to complete. The IEP is not meant to hinder the student's education, but rather it is there to support it.

wavebreakmedia/Shutterstock.com

How Student Progress Will Be Reported?

Brett's IEP indicates *how often* the goal will be reported, which is biweekly, but it does not specifically indicate who is responsible for making those reports. Generally, this will be reported by the person responsible for the goal. In Brett's case, it would be the special education teacher. How will this be handled if the regular education teacher and the special education teacher are both responsible for the goal? Either teacher could make the progress report, so that makes it critical that the decision and identification of who will be responsible for the goal be made and documented in order to ensure that the progress gets reported.

Short-Term Benchmarks/Objectives

In the case of short-term benchmarks/objectives, Brett's teachers will most likely need to work collaboratively to ensure that these goals are met. Let us take a closer look at Brett's benchmarks/objectives below.

Short-Term Objectives or Benchmarks, if necessary: or circle if N/A
Objective/Benchmark One: Given a literacy text, Brett will read aloud and explain the author's main idea and purpose in a writing sample, based on a rubric, in three out of four trials by December 13, 2022. Assessment method: Teacher observation and writing rubric
Objective/Benchmark Two: Given a literary text, Brett will define the relationships between and among elements of literature: characters, plot, setting, tone, point of view, and theme in three out of four trails by March 13, 2023. Assessment method: Writing elements rubric
Objective/Benchmark Three: Given a literary text, Brett will analyze how an author's specific word choices and syntax achieve special effects and support the author's purpose. The literary text will be read, and Brett will correctly answer 80% of the questions pertaining to the text in three out of four trials as graded by end-of-novel test. Assessment method: End of novel test

Though this is only a sample of Brett's objectives/benchmarks, we can see that he was provided with three different benchmark goals and assessments. Notice that in the top bar of the chart, there is a place to indicate "N/A." This means that, according to his PLAAFP, he does not require short-term objectives or benchmarks.

Notice that the objectives/benchmarks also contain the ABCD elements in the measurable annual goals. The difference is that the measurable annual goals are meant to be accomplished in the next school year while the short-term objectives/benchmarks are meant to help the student achieve the measurable annual goals.

Assessments

Looking at the objectives and benchmarks above, we see that they require that the student be assessed as well. Note that these are specific assessments, such as "End of novel test." These assessment statements do not make a general statement such as "worksheet." Assessments need to be specific in order to ensure that the measurable annual goals and the objectives and benchmarks correspond with one another and actually measure and assess the information pertaining to the goal. For Brett's first measurable annual goal, he will be assessed in multiple ways including teacher observation, writing rubric, writing elements rubric, and an end of novel test. Assessing in a variety of assessment formats allows for a stronger representation of the student's overall achievement.

Least Restrictive Environment

Accommodations/Modifications

Looking at Brett's accommodations, we see that both the LRE and Accommodations/Modifications are indicated on the same chart. These two elements are not indicated on every IEP, but for Brett's IEP, it makes it easy to decipher who is responsible for each element. The special education and general education teacher will be responsible for all of the accommodations/modifications. This is a situation when collaboration and a team approach to the IPE process will play out. If the IEP team leader has spent time cultivating a healthy relationship with the general education teacher, it will be easier to work together to ensure that Brett is appropriately assessed by the appropriate person.

Accommodations/Modifications					
Accommodations/ Modifications	Delivery Recommendations	Least Restrictive Environment	Frequency	Duration	Services Begin
Tests and assignments read aloud to student	As needed	Special education classroom	Daily	During instructional class time or during tests	9/23/22
Support for organizational skills	Agenda checked daily by teacher at end of class	Special and general education classroom	Conclusion of every class	Throughout the school day	9/23/22
Refocusing and redirection	Brett requires assistance in attending to classroom activities	Special and general education classroom	Daily	Throughout the school day	9/23/22
Strategic Seating	Brett focuses best when placed in close proximity to the teacher near the front of the room	Special and general education classroom			9/23/22
Copy of class notes	As needed	Special and general education classroom			9/23/22
Extended time for assessments	As needed	Special and general education classroom	As needed	During assessments	9/23/22

Below is an example of a measurable annual goal with appropriate names added to indicate the person responsible for the goal. Identifying specific goals and who is responsible is important in order to ensure that the student's goals are met.

<table>
<tr><th colspan="3">Annual Goal: One</th></tr>
<tr><td colspan="3">Goal: Reading
In 12 months, Brett will read and exhibit comprehension of the ninth grade text, including prose, drama, poetry, and content area subject text in 80% of given opportunities, as measured biweekly on teacher-devised tests or text worksheets.</td></tr>
<tr><td colspan="3">Standard of learning related to this goal: Virginia Standard 9.4
The student will read, comprehend, and analyze a variety of literacy texts including narratives, narrative nonfiction, poetry, and drama.</td></tr>
<tr><td colspan="3">Progress toward this goal will be measured: (Check all that apply)</td></tr>
<tr><td>✓ Tests and Quizzes
___ Standardized Test
___ Norm Referenced Test
___ Other Assessment</td><td>✓ Classwork
___ Projects
___ Homework
✓ Participation</td><td>___ Written Report
✓ Observation
___ Checklist
___ Other</td></tr>
<tr><td colspan="3">Progress toward this goal will be reported:</td></tr>
<tr><td colspan="3">Biweekly</td></tr>
<tr><td colspan="3">Short-Term Objectives or Benchmarks, if necessary: or circle if N/A</td></tr>
<tr><td colspan="3">Objective/Benchmark One: Kelly Garman, Special Education Teacher
Given a literacy text, Brett will read aloud and explain the author's main idea and purpose in a writing sample based, on a rubric in three out of four trials by December 13, 2022.

Assessment method: Teacher observation and writing rubric</td></tr>
<tr><td colspan="3">Objective/Benchmark Two: Stuart Fisher, General Education Teacher
Given a literary text, Brett will define the relationships between and among elements of literature: characters, plot, setting, tone, point of view, and theme in three out of four trails by March 13, 2023.

Assessment method: Writing elements rubric</td></tr>
<tr><td colspan="3">Objective/Benchmark Three: Kelly Garman, Special Education Teacher
Given a literary text, Brett will analyze how an author's specific word choices and syntax achieve special effects and support the author's purpose. The literary text will be read, and Brett will correctly answer 80% of the questions pertaining to the text in three out of four trials as graded by end of novel test.

Assessment method: End of novel test</td></tr>
</table>

Related Services

On the Related Services page below, there is a column to indicate who is responsible for the implementation and delivery of services. The only service that Brett is receiving is for Speech/Language Therapy, and Mr. Greer is responsible for that service. You may recall that Mr. Greer requested to be excused from the IEP meeting in order to have surgery. It is highly likely that you will run into a situation where the person responsible for a part of the IEP will not be able to provide the required element, such as in this case. How should this be handled? There is not a one-size-fits-all answer to this question, as all cases will need to be determined on an individual basis. However, it is important to remember that this service, by law, has to be lawfully provided to Brett, and it is expected that he received it. If Mr. Greer is not able to provide the service, then a short-term substitute or other credentialed Speech/Language Therapist will need to be secured to offer Brett the service he needs to ensure that his rights to a Free Appropriate Public Education (FAPE) are not denied.

Related Services

	Related Services					
Service	Service Delivery Recommendations	Person Responsible	Instructional Setting	Frequency	Duration	Services Begin
Speech/ Language Therapy	Small group (5:1)	Mr. Greer	Therapy room	Twice weekly	40 min	Beginning 10/19/22
~ Identify, if applicable, class size, language (if other than English), group or individual services, direct and/or indirect consultant teacher services, or other service delivery recommendations.						

Assessments

The Assessments section of the IEP does not have a location to indicate who is responsible for assessing Brett. It is oftentimes assumed that this will be the responsibility of the special education teacher. However, it is never a good idea to assume when it comes to ensuring that the IEP is followed correctly and that the student's rights to a FAPE are not denied. Once again, even though there is not a place to indicate which person is responsible for assessing the student, it is a best practice to write down who is responsible for this section.

Liberty Academic School

Individualized Education Plan
Assessments

Kelly Garman

Individual testing accommodations, specific to the student's disability and needs, must be used consistently by the student in the recommended educational program and in the administration of district-wide assessments of the student achievement and, in accordance with department policy, state assessments of student achievement as indicated below.

Testing Accommodation	Condition	Implementation Recommendations
Describe the type, length, and purpose of the test upon which the use of testing accommodations in conditioned, if applicable. Identify the amount of extended time, type of setting, and so on, specific to testing accommodations, if applicable.		
• Time and a half extended time • Administered in special education classroom • Use of a computer	For all quizzes/tests: Read aloud to student Use of computer	Tests administered in a small group (3-5 students) Computer used to read to the student and/or to type answers

Narrative Explanation of Assessment Decision
Due to Brett's specific learning disability, he is given extended time on assignments and tests. He is easily distracted and thus will benefit from being away from distractions and allowed to complete assignments and tests with a small group of students or in a one-on-one setting. The use of computer aides with specially designed instruction such as web-based instructions and the use of earphones, will be allowed.

Participation in State and District-wide Assessments

__✓__ The student will participate in the same state and district-wide assessments administered to the general education students.

______ The student will participate in an alternate assessment on a state or district-wide assessment of student achievement. If checked, identify the alternate assessment below.

____

Alternate Assessment

Note the reason the student will not participate in the same state and district-wide assessments administered to the general education students and why the specific alternative assessment is appropriate.

Transition Plan

The IEP team leader is responsible for the Transition Plan in most cases. On Brett's IEP, there is a chart indicating the Transition Plan Activities required for Brett and an indication of which person is responsible for each item. This clearly states who is responsible. Since the column listing the persons responsible for each item includes more than one person, it is a good idea to be more specific and indicate the precise role of each person for each service/activity.

Transition Plan Activities		
Needed Activities to Facilitate the Student's Movement from School to Post-School Activities	**Service/Activity**	**School/District/Agency Responsible**
Instruction	~ Review high school course syllabi for class preferences, with a focus on courses/electives in auto mechanics ~ Participate in general education elective courses and notify teachers of accommodations/modifications ~ Participate in IEP meetings and communicate personal accommodations, assist in the development of goals, and articulate personal modifications needed in an educational setting ~ Manage time schedules for daily and long-term assignments/projects	~ Student, parent, guidance counselor ~ Student, general education teacher, special education teacher ~ Student, parent, general education teacher, special education teacher, guidance counselor, psychologist ~ Student, special education teacher
Related Services	Speech/Language Therapy to improve communication skills	~ Student, Speech/Language Therapist
Community Experiences	Participate in community service activities/internship through auto mechanics course	~ Student, general education teacher
Development of Employment and other Post-High-School Adult Living Objectives	Create a profile on Career Zone to research and further refine career preferences in auto mechanics	~ Student, special education teacher, guidance counselor
Daily Living Skills (if applicable)	Considering Brett's current levels of performance, Daily Living Skills (DLS) is not needed at this time	N/A
Functional Vocational Assessment (if applicable)	Considering Brett's current levels of performance, Functional Vocational Assessment (FVA) is not needed at this time	N/A

Though a list of do's and don'ts for implementing an IEP is helpful, it is an educator's character that will make the most difference when going through the IEP process. The Bible says "Be always humble, gentle, and patient. Show your love by being tolerant with one another" (Eph. 4:2, Good News Translation). This verse is especially helpful to remember when working collaboratively with a team of people. Every member will bring different experiences and varying degrees of education to the meeting and every member should be valued. Even when team members disagree, the situation should be handled with dignity. Proverbs 3:3 says "Do not let kindness and truth leave you; Bind them around your neck, Write them on the tablet of your heart" (New American Standard Bible). Imagine how much more pleasant and productive an IEP meeting, and the entire process, could be if every member approached the IEP process with this attitude. The importance of grace cannot be overstated here. Modeling the values of Christ in establishing a positive student-teacher relationship is still one of the most effective ways to impact a student's success.

In Ephesians 4:29, Paul instructs us, "Let no corrupting talk come out of your mouths, but only such as is good for building up, as fits the occasion, that it may give grace to those who hear" (English Standard Version). Christians are called to speak the truth, in love, to those they encounter. Words should be used for the uplifting of others and to demonstrate grace, whether deserved or not. Teachers have the power to use their words to encourage and uplift their students and IEP team members. When frustrated, it can be easy to use words to lash out and tear down students or colleagues in the process. However, taking the time to slow down and consider our words has the potential to propel relationships and can be powerful tools that are used to enhance the success of each student. Trials will come but let me encourage you to handle them in a Christ-like manner. "Rejoice in hope, be patient in tribulation, be constant in prayer" (Rom. 12:12). Spending time with the Lord in prayer is what will set your leadership skills apart from others.

© Monkey Business Images/Shutterstock.com

Conclusion

Character and discernment are such integral parts of the IEP process and, as an educator, you will be required to make many, many decisions for your students throughout the day, week, and year. Once again, this is why prayer should be such an important part of the IEP process. It takes wisdom and discernment to make these decisions. In the hustle and bustle of the school day, it is easy to lose sight of what is best for the student and to focus on the path of least resistance. Sometimes what is easier in the moment is not what is best in the long run for the student. The Bible tells us to value others above ourselves and to look to their interests rather than our own (Phil. 2:1–4). This verse epitomizes the teachers I know, as most choose to spend their lives serving their students.

As stated in Chapter 4 and reiterated here, Romans 12:4–8 applies to the collaboration that is needed among IEP team members to provide the best possible education for each student.

> For just as each of us had one body with many members, and these members do not all have the same function, so in Christ we, though many, form one body and each member belongs to all the others. We have different gifts, according to the grace given to each of us. If your gift is prophesying, then prophesy in accordance with your faith; if it is serving, then serve; if it is teaching, then teach; if it is to encourage, then give encouragement; if it is giving, then give generously; if it is to lead, do it diligently; if it is to show mercy, do it cheerfully.

This verse is a great reminder to us to do the best we are able to do based on the gifts and talents that the Lord has blessed us with. Though I can provide you with a lot of scripture to try to convict or convince you, the best thing I can do for you and your students is to encourage you to spend time in the Bible yourself; that is where true life-changing interactions occur. Spend time with the Lord every single day, and He will guide your steps. He will provide the wisdom and discernment you need in order to build healthy life-changing IEPs for your students.

I pray that this book has provided you with some spiritual guidance for planning, writing, and implementing an IEP. My hope is that you feel empowered to approach this IEP process with confidence as you seek the Lord's guidance and wisdom. Let me end with the beautiful verse of scripture:

"The Lord make His face shine upon you and be gracious to you; the Lord turn His face toward you and give you peace" (Num. 6:25–26).

Chapter Highlights

IDEA regulations require that "as soon as possible following development of the IEP, special education and related services are made available to the child in accordance with the child's IEP" (34 C.F.R. §300.323[c]).

The student's IEP must be readily available to each teacher, related services provider, or any other service provider responsible for its implementation (34 C.F.R. §300.323[d][1]).

It is a best practice to provide a copy of the IEP to all responsible parties and to document the receipt of the information by each recipient.

According to IDEA,

> Schools must ensure that every staff person responsible for implementing the IEP is "informed of his or her specific responsibilities related to implementing the child's IEP; and the specific accommodations, modifications, or supports that must be provided for the child in accordance with the IEP." (34 C.F.R. §300.323[d][2])

The reason the IEP was written with observable and measurable goals is so that educational growth be documented, and to some degree quantified.

The IEP team leader is responsible for the Transition Plan in most cases.

Modeling the values of Christ in establishing a positive student-teacher relationship is still one of the most effective ways to impact a student's success.

Teachers have the power to use their words to encourage and uplift their students and IEP team members.

"Rejoice in hope, be patient in tribulation, be constant in prayer" (Rom. 12:12). Spending time with the Lord in prayer is what will set your leadership skills apart from others.

"The Lord make His face shine upon you and be gracious to you; the Lord turn His face toward you and give you peace" (Num. 6:25–26).

Chapter Review Questions

1. List and explain the steps involved in implementing an IEP.
2. What are the elements of an IEP, and what are included in each of those elements?
3. Write out five different possible action items for an IEP, and identify who could be responsible for each of those action items.
4. Based on your current school or the grade level you intend to teach, write at least one goal and the benchmark and assessment(s) for reaching that goal.

Additional Resources

- For additional legal information on implementing an IEP: http://www.ksde.org/Portals/0/SES/legal/conf14/B2-JMartin-IEPImplementation.pdf

CHAPTER 9

Functional Behavior Assessment

Learning Outcomes

After reading this chapter, you should be able to:

- ❑ Explain the law regarding student behavior and IEPs
- ❑ Define a Functional Behavior Assessment
- ❑ Define a Behavioral Intervention Plan
- ❑ Explain a target behavior
- ❑ Describe a measurable and observable target behavior
- ❑ Discuss data relevant to a target behavior
- ❑ Write a hypothesis statement

Vocabulary

- ❑ Functional Behavior Assessment
- ❑ Behavioral Intervention Plan
- ❑ Target behavior

Student behavior can either enhance or inhibit learning. When student behavior interferes with the learning process, the situation must be remedied. In some cases, a student may only need a verbal reprimand to correct his or her behavior. However, in other circumstances, student behavior may be extreme and may warrant additional measures to correct the behavior. Some behaviors may be harmful to self or others. As an educator, it is important to understand when to intervene and how to intervene to best serve all students. In this chapter, you will learn the difference between a Functional Behavior Assessment (FBA) and a Behavior Intervention Plan (BIP), as well as how the two are related. Additionally, you will learn when and how to complete an FBA and a BIP. This chapter is intended to provide a detailed overview of an FBA and a BIP. It is not intended to fully train the reader to engage in these activities without further proper training.

The Law

As noted in chapter one of this book, PL 94-142, Individuals with Disabilities Education Act (IDEA) (1997, 2004) was enacted to ensure that all children with disabilities receive a free public education "to meet their unique needs and prepare them for further education, employment, and independent living" (APA, 2015). The IDEA Amendments of 1997 require that the relationship between behavior and academic achievement must be *acted upon*. In other words, behavior issues must be considered, and resolved, in the academic process. Individual Education Plans (IEPs) must address behaviors that distract from the learning process and may require an FBA and a BIP that utilizes positive behavior supports: the key word being "positive."

According to IDEA:

- The IEP team must address any behavior(s) that impeded learning.
- The IEP team must meet within 10 days of a disciplinary infraction to formulate an FBA to record evidence to be used to create a BIP or to review and revise an existing plan.
- States are required to provide training related to developing and implementing positive intervention strategies for faculty and staff.

The IEP team must address behaviors that impeded learning whether it is the learning of the student with a disability or other students. Behaviors that impede learning must be addressed. When a student engages in behaviors that impede the learning process, the IEP team is then responsible for devising a plan of action to target the specific behaviors and to try to eliminate the target behaviors using positive behavior supports. Teachers and staff who work with students, such as general education teachers, special education teachers, and paraprofessionals, should be provided with proper training to engage in the FBA and BIP process to ensure that targeted behaviors are corrected utilizing positive intervention strategies.

What is an FBA?

An **FBA** is an assessment of unacceptable behavior(s) and requires information and evidence to determine the cause or purpose of a behavior. The FBA is typically conducted before a BIP is written. The FBA is highly individualized, and the format of an FBA varies greatly. The information collected should provide evidence and understanding regarding the behavior, including why the behavior may occur and in what context it typically occurs. The FBA is said to identify the ABC. The ABC is the Antecedent, Behavior, and the Consequences. The Antecedent is what precedes the behavior. The behavior is the target behavior that needs to be eliminated or changed. And the consequences are what the student is getting from the target behavior and can either be positive or negative. This information and supporting evidence are then utilized by the IEP team to write a BIP to help correct the behavior.

Below is an example of a blank FBA. In this chapter, we will complete this document to further your understanding of the FBA process. As you read the form, note the categories of information that are necessary to complete the FBA.

Functional Behavior Assessment Summary

Student: ____________________ DOB: ____________________
School: ____________________ Grade: ____________________
Date: ____________________ Assessor: ____________________

Data Sources:
- ☐ Observations (settings: classroom, lunchroom)
- ☐ Teacher interview
- ☐ Student interview
- ☐ Parent contact
- ☐ Other____________

Description of Behaviors: (use concrete terms, provide specific descriptors of behaviors)

Frequency of Behaviors:

Duration of Behaviors:

Intensity: (Impact of the target behavior on students, peers, and the learning environment)

Setting: (Where does the behavior occur? Include time of day, with specific individuals, structured or unstructured setting, etc.)

Triggers: (Identify circumstances that appear to begin the behavior.)

Consequences: (what is the response after the behavior has occurred?)

Educational Impact: (How does the behavior impact learning for self and others?)

Strengths/Rcsources

Student:

School:

Family:

Community:

Function of the Student's Behavior: (What purpose does the behavior serve for the student?)

- ☐ To regulate affect (i.e., anxiety, anger, depression, lack of self-esteem)
- ☐ To gain attention
- ☐ To gain control
- ☐ To avoid/escape settings, tasks, individuals, situations
- ☐ To obtain specific object or activities
- ☐ To avoid/escape internal distractions (psychological/physical/neurological difficulties)
- ☐ To communicate needs or desires (lacks effective communication skills)
- ☐ Other ___________

Observational Data:

Hypothesis Statement:

Suggested Recommendation/Replacement Behavior(s):

Positive Behavior Supports Attempted:

It is important to differentiate the FBA from the BIP. As a reminder, the FBA is a Functional Behavior Assessment and the BIP is the Behavior Intervention Plan. Typically, the FBA is completed first and it is used to determine the BIP.

What is a BIP?

A **BIP** is a Behavior Intervention Plan written to address specific target behavior(s) and includes positive interventions, strategies, and supports. Much like the IEP, the BIP is written by a team made up of school faculty and parents who desire to see a student's behavior change. The behavior must be specifically named and is often called the **target behavior**. The BIP is used to encourage appropriate positive behaviors and to eliminate targeted negative behaviors. Though the BIP usually follows an FBA, it is not a legal requirement.

An FBA is an approach to changing behaviors that encompasses a variety of strategies to determine the causes of a target behavior and to identify the best strategies to change the behaviors. FBAs focus on detecting biological, social, and environmental factors that may cause the target behavior. This approach is different from other approaches since it seeks to address the cause of the behavior and not just eliminate the behavior. Determining the cause of the target behavior may help to eliminate the target behavior permanently, whereas simply trying to eliminate a specific behavior punitively may only temporarily eliminate the behavior. The goal of an FBA and a BIP is to permanently eliminate or change the target behavior by determining what is causing the behavior and by utilizing positive behavior supports and strategies. The FBA serves as the analysis of the problem. The BIP serves as the plan of action to eliminate or change the behavior.

The FBA serves as the analysis of the problem. The BIP serves as the plan of action to eliminate or change the behavior.

How to Write an FBA

An FBA contains information regarding the target behavior. There are essentially four basic components of the FBA including:

1. Definition of the target behavior
2. Detailed measure of the target behavior
3. Data relevant to the target behavior
4. Hypothesis statement and recommendations

An FBA needs to provide details regarding a student's behavior. Enough details need to be provided that a team may understand the behavior and analyze the data to try to determine a plan for correcting the behavior. Possible questions that may be addressed on the FBA include, but are not limited to, the following:

What happened?
When did it happen?
Where did it happen?
How often did it happen?
How long did it last?
How intense was the behavior?
Who observed the behavior?
Who was present when it occurred?
Who was involved in the incident?
What is the antecedent to the behavior?
What was the outcome?
What is the educational impact?

Components of an FBA

Let us look at the four components of an FBA in more detail. Recall that FBAs and BIPs vary greatly. Below is one way to write an FBA, but it is not the only way.

1. Definition of the Target Behavior

A definition of the target behavior that needs to be changed should be included in the FBA. Enough detail must be provided to help devise a plan for change. You should provide details regarding what the student is doing that is interfering with the learning process, whose learning is impacted, and whether or not the behavior is causing harm to the student and/or others. Below is an example of a definition of a target behavior appropriate for an FBA.

Description of Target Behaviors:

Noncompliant and disruptive behavior: Brett does not often comply with teacher directions or classroom rules. He is oftentimes disruptive to the learning environment by calling out and being out of his seat. Brett does not always stop the inappropriate behavior when he is told to stop. At times, he has demonstrated argumentative behavior with the teacher. Brett has an active body and has a hard time sitting still and remaining on task. He rocks back and forth and bounces, and he is frequently fiddling with a pencil sharpener during class time. He requires multiple prompts to stay on task and becomes very easily distracted by things around him and things in his desk.

Lacks appropriate social interactions: Brett also has trouble engaging appropriately and positively with his classmates. He oftentimes misjudges the intentions of others, and his efforts to interact playfully are not always effective or well received.

2. Detailed Measure of the Target Behavior

The behavior must be measurable and observable. For example, it is not sufficient to say that "Brett is mean to his classmates." This is not specifically measurable and observable. It would be more appropriate to say, "Brett hit two classmates in the head with a spoon while standing in line to get lunch." Much like goals written in an IEP, the measure of the behavior needs to include details.

As you can see, a lot of details are required for an FBA in order for a proper analysis of the behavior to occur. Generally speaking, the more detail that is provided, the more clues there are to understand the root cause of the behavior. Understanding the cause of the behavior will help the IEP team to determine an effective plan that utilizes positive behavior interventions and strategies to eliminate the behavior. Below is an example of the measure of a target behavior.

Frequency of Behaviors:

Brett's behaviors occur daily and can vary depending on events that occurred prior to him entering the classroom. Specific tasks that are challenging to Brett, such as reading and worksheets, can also trigger negative responses from him.

Duration of Behaviors:

Depending on the response to Brett's behavior, escalation can occur, or Brett can be redirected at times. If Brett's behavior escalates, he can demonstrate and engage in negative behaviors for an entire class period.

Intensity:

Brett's negative behaviors and off-task behaviors can oftentimes keep him from engaging in the learning process. Second, Brett also expressed that he has trouble making friends, and his negative classroom behaviors have made establishing and maintaining friendships more difficult.

Setting:

Brett has struggled and expressed frustration in a variety of settings. Socially, he has difficulty in unstructured settings such as physical education (PE), recess, lunch, and the bathroom. Academically, he struggles in the classroom to sit still and conform to expectations. Brett has demonstrated challenging behaviors in all settings throughout the school day.

Triggers:

Directing Brett to complete written work can be a trigger. Writing is challenging for him. If Brett has to sit quietly, he will likely struggle to keep his body still. Public correction may also be a trigger for negative behaviors.

Brett appears to have great difficulty keeping himself focused and quiet when the class is reviewing work that he already understands. He works at a faster pace than most of his classmates, and because he "checks out" when other students need extra explanation, he gets caught up in distracting activities such as talking, fiddling in his desk, and moving around.

Working beyond 8 to 10 min will likely trigger off-task behavior for Brett. His maximum work span and attention span are about 10 min. Beyond that timeframe, negative distracting behaviors are triggered.

Consequences:

For the most part, Brett's behavior is being ignored in the classroom, when possible. He is being redirected to appropriate behaviors when doing so results in minimal distraction to other students. Brett has been sent to the assistant principal to discuss his behavior when his behavior has become extreme and disruptive to the learning process of other students.

Educational Impact:
Brett's behavior is preventing him from fully engaging in the learning process. At times, his behavior also distracts his classmates from fully engaging in the learning process.

3. Data Relevant to the Target Behavior

Further data must be collected and assessed. This data may be solicited from teachers, students, parents, or administrators when possible and appropriate. Data may include the documents such as office discipline referrals, observations, health records, checklists, or questionnaires, as suitable for the situation. Below is an example of data that may be relevant to the target behavior.

Strengths/Resources

Student:
Brett can be very honest at times. He can admit when he makes a mistake when he is given some time to process the situation. Brett has demonstrated the ability to hold himself accountable for his own actions despite his tendency to blame others for causing the initial problem. Brett participates readily and actively in morning and afternoon check-in as part of his daily experiences at school. He is willing to work on a new goal, and he is honest about acknowledging when he cannot meet his goal or did not try his hardest.
School:
Brett receives services under an IEP as a student with attention deficit hyperactivity disorder. He is placed in a co-taught classroom and receives a lot of cueing and support from the special education teacher. Brett meets regularly with the school psychologist for short check-ins and regular processing sessions after an incident and he has been demonstrating honest and positive affect in his sessions.
Family:
Brett's mother is very supportive of her son and recognizes that he struggles with making good choices and that social skills are not a strength for him. She openly communicates with the school and has been supportive of efforts to support her son.
Community:
Brett sees an outside counselor on a regular basis. His mom picks him up from school to take him. At this time, the counseling experience is reported to be positive and somewhat helpful.

Function of the Student's Behavior:

- ☑ To regulate affect (i.e., anxiety, anger, depression, lack of self-esteem)
- ☑ To gain attention
- ☐ To gain control
- ☑ To avoid/escape settings, tasks, individuals, situations
- ☐ To obtain specific object or activities
- ☐ To avoid/escape internal distractions (psychological/physical/neurological difficulties)
- ☐ To communicate needs or desires (lacks effective communication skills)
- ☐ Other ____________

Observational Data:

Brett was observed in his language arts class. When given a motivator to finish his quiz and earn iPad time, he worked steadily for 8 min. He turned in the quiz and waited patiently for the iPad to be given to him. He was told he needed to wait by his teacher, and he coped with the delayed gratification and was able to sit fairly quietly. He put his head down for a couple of minutes, and then began fiddling with a pencil sharpener. He did remain in his seat and was mostly quiet.

During the next part of the observation, Brett was expected to sit and listen to instructions on the country project that his class was working on. He was able to stay seated, and once the kids were given the go-ahead to start working, Brett was allowed to earn his iPad time. He transitioned from the iPad and began working on his project without incident. He was eager to start on his poster like many of the other students, but he had not collected his facts yet and was a bit behind. It was hard for him to refrain from working on the hands-on portion of the project, but his teacher directed him to go back to his seat and finish finding his facts. He insisted he had found them, and she told him to go to his seat and raise his hand and wait for her to come check it as she did with all the other students. Brett complied and went back to his seat and raised his hand. The teacher finished working with another student, and then came to Brett. She gave him some feedback and required him to gather a little more information. Brett did not appear to get upset. He went back to the computer to look for more facts.

In math class, Brett was able to compute math facts quickly. His brain works quicker than his ability to record his processing. Brett expressed this to the observer. He may benefit from some self-paced math on a computer where he can be challenged at his level and where he can work at a speed that keeps him engaged and learning.

Brett often draws pictures when he is upset. He does a good job of choosing colors that represent his mood. Most of his drawings show a combination of different colors that represent emotions. Anger is most often included, along with sad. He will frequently include small sections of green to indicate happy and sometimes other colors, such as orange and yellow, to indicate some struggle. Brett seems to demonstrate feeling better after he draws.

Brett was observed having a facilitated interaction with a peer. The other student was asked to provide some feedback to Brett. The student shared honestly that he feels kids would like to be friends with Brett but when he does not follow the rules, or he is disrespectful to the teacher, he is going to be judged more negatively. Brett was asked how he feels about the student. He replied, "I like him because he is nice, but I don't like him because he's not my friend." Brett became emotional when he later admitted that he has a lot of trouble making friends.

4. Hypothesis Statement Regarding the Behavior

The fourth component of an FBA is the hypothesis statement, sometimes called the summary. The hypothesis statement is determined and written by the IEP team member(s) and is an analysis of the data collection and information presented to understand the function or purpose of the target behavior. Below is an example of a hypothesis statement.

Hypothesis Statement:

Brett has a hard time keeping his body still. He also does not always make appropriate choices. His motivation for misbehavior seems to be driven to get attention or avoid nonpreferred tasks. Brett needs to stay engaged and kept busy. He computes math in his head and has a hard time slowing down his brain enough to show his work. It is difficult for him to wait while others are still processing the information that comes easily to him.

Brett's fine motor skills are poor based on work samples. His writing mechanics are not at grade level. His writing content appears to be good, but he lacks organizational skills. Brett may produce more work if he uses speech-to-text on assignments and assessments that are not assessing the skill of writing.

Graphic organizers would be very useful in helping Brett organize his thoughts and navigate him through the writing process.

Brett frequently seeks attention in a negative way. He admits it and recognizes it later. Brett processes extremely well and has been able to be honest.

Brett's efforts to make friends and connect with peers are frequently the wrong type of efforts. He tries to show off and to be silly, and he intentionally breaks the rules, but is not making the connection because these behaviors are not peer-approved and are causing him further isolation from social relationships.

Similarly, in the classroom, it appears that Brett is trying to impress his classmates, and he wants to be accepted. His misguided efforts keep him from making friends.

Brett's mix of emotions and his lack of emotional control and self-regulation make it a difficult mix of feelings that results in challenging behaviors. This oftentimes results in poor behavioral choices and outbursts.

Suggested Recommendation/Replacement Behavior(s):

Providing scheduled breaks for Brett during the day and structuring his work with a numbered list of goals may increase his overall motivation and work production. This model should be coupled with motivators that he can earn from a list of options.

Brett is highly motivated by a ticket system where the teacher sends home positive notes to his parents to reward his efforts. He is able to process honesty and he can admit when he has not earned a privilege.

Brett needs to learn to employ some coping strategies such as writing about his feelings in a feelings journal or drawing a picture if he is not feeling well. Oftentimes, when Brett has an opportunity to express how he is feeling in words or pictures, he is able to "move on," and make better choices. He responds very well to specific guidance and directions.

Brett's "infractions" need to be processed within a neutral environment when he is calm. A tracking sheet of negative behavior choices may be helpful to assist him in recognizing where he made a poor choice. Providing positive choices as an alternative may help him to choose wisely the next time.

Morning check-ins are recommended to help identify Brett's mood and set a behavioral goal for the day. Brett may need to have scheduled breaks throughout the day if his behavior begins to decline. Building in breaks after 10 min of work may allow Brett the time he needs to move, which should allow him to reset so that he can begin to work again.

Use of a timer or stopwatch to help Brett use his time more efficiently is recommended.

Use of a prompt counting card to help Brett keep track of his prompts during the day and try to earn independent work-time credits may help him keep this as a goal and track his progress. A simple index card with tally marks should be sufficient.

Blended learning style is recommended so that he may be challenged.

Asking Brett to restate the expectations and to demonstrate them may be more effective than a reprimand or verbal correction.

Positive Behavior Supports Attempted:

Earning "stars" for good behavior (PBIS)

Sending to the assistant principal

Ignoring the behavior

Parent contact

Staff meeting with parents

Discussion

Warnings

Summary

The first step to conducting an FBA is to define the target behavior. Recall that the behavior must be measurable and observable. In order to define the behavior specifically, it may be necessary to observe the student in multiple locations and over multiple instances. This may also require that you discuss the observed behavior with other teachers who may have also experienced the behavior.

After the behavior has been defined, the IEP team may devise a plan to conduct the FBA. This plan is intended to collect enough data to determine the root cause of the target behavior. Then, positive interventions and strategies may be determined to change the target behavior.

A thoroughly developed and implemented FBA will identify the triggers that contribute to the target behavior. Determining the context of the behavior requires data that are collected using a variety of sources of information. Data from one source of information is rarely, if ever, sufficient information to devise an informed plan to eliminate the target behavior.

An FBA provides valuable information to the IEP team who is then charged with devising and implementing a BIP to change behavior by using positive behavior supports.

Chapter Highlights

PL 94-142, IDEA (1997, 2004) was enacted to ensure that all children with disabilities receive a free public education "to meet their unique needs and prepare them for further education, employment, and independent living" (APA, 2015).

The IDEA Amendments of 1997 require that the relationship between behavior and academic achievement must be *acted upon*.

IEPs must address behaviors that distract from the learning process and may require an FBA and a BIP that utilizes positive behavior supports: the key word being "positive."

According to IDEA:

- The IEP team must address any behavior(s) that impeded learning.
- The IEP team must meet within 10 days of a disciplinary infraction to formulate an FBA to record evidence to be used to create a BIP or to review and revise an existing plan.
- States are required to provide training related to developing and implementing positive intervention strategies for faculty and staff.

The IEP team must address behaviors that impeded learning whether it is the learning of the student with a disability or other students.

Teachers and staff who work with students, such as general education teachers, special education teachers, and paraprofessionals, should be provided with proper training to engage in the FBA and BIP processes to ensure that targeted behaviors are corrected utilizing positive intervention strategies.

An FBA is an assessment of unacceptable behavior(s) and requires information and evidence to determine the cause or purpose of a behavior.

The BIP is used to encourage appropriate positive behaviors and to eliminate targeted negative behaviors.

The goal of an FBA and a BIP is to permanently eliminate or change the target behavior by determining what is causing the behavior and by utilizing positive behavior supports and strategies.

The FBA serves as the analysis of the problem.

The BIP serves as the plan of action to eliminate or change the behavior.

Chapter Review Questions

1. Describe a Functional Behavior Assessment.
2. Describe a Behavior Intervention Plan.
3. How does an FBI inform a BIP?
4. List the four components of a FBA.
5. Define a target behavior and provide an example.
6. When writing a BIP, describe the types of strategies used to change behaviors?

Additional Resources

- Rodriguez, J., & Murawski, W. (2022). *Special education law and policy: From foundation to application*. Plural Publishing, Inc.

CHAPTER 10

Behavior Intervention Plan

Learning Outcomes

After reading this chapter, you should be able to:

- ❑ Define a Behavioral Intervention Plan (BIP)
- ❑ Write a goal for a BIP
- ❑ Describe the setting events, triggers, and context for target behaviors
- ❑ Determine a hypothetical function of behaviors
- ❑ Write preventions, consequences, and follow-ups for a target behavior
- ❑ Describe interventions and persons responsible for implementation

Vocabulary

- ❑ Functional Behavior Assessment
- ❑ Behavioral Intervention Plan
- ❑ Target behavior
- ❑ Hypothetical Function of Behaviors

As noted in the previous chapter, a Functional Behavior Assessment (FBA) is an assessment of target behavior(s) and requires information and evidence to determine the cause or purpose of a behavior. This is typically conducted before a Behavioral Intervention Plan (BIP) is written. The FBA is highly individualized, and the format of an FBA varies greatly. The information collected should provide evidence and understanding regarding the behavior, including why the behavior may occur and in what context it typically occurs. This information and evidence are then utilized by the Individualized Education Plan (IEP) team to write a BIP to help eliminate or change the behavior.

Behavior Intervention Plans may be found in a variety of formats, but the elements of the BIP are essentially the same. The IEP team will meet to develop a new BIP plan or to revise an old plan. The BIP should include positive strategies, interventions, and supports to address the target behaviors. Information collected during the FBA should be used to determine the BIP.

Information should have been collected from persons who spend time with the student such as the general education teacher, special education teacher, students, parents, and so on. Collecting evidence and data from those persons who work most closely with the student may increase the accuracy of the data used to determine the BIP. Recall that the goal of the BIP is to determine the root cause of the behavior in an effort to permanently eliminate or change target behaviors.

Below is an example of a blank BIP. In this chapter, we will complete this document to further your understanding of the BIP process. As you read the form, note the categories of information that are necessary to complete the BIP.

Behavior Intervention Plan

Student:	**DOB:**
School:	**Grade:**
Date:	**Case Manager:**

Goal for Plan:

Setting Events, Triggers, Contexts (Antecedents):

Hypothetical Function of Behaviors:

Behavior Intervention Plan

Target Behavior:	**Prevention:** **Consequence:** **Follow-up:**

Target Behavior:	**Prevention:** **Consequence:** **Follow-up:**

Target Behavior:	Prevention: Consequence: Follow-up:

Target Behavior:	Prevention: Consequence: Follow-up:

Target Behavior:	Prevention: Consequence: Follow-up:

Interventions:	Person(s) Responsible for Implementing Intervention:

Review Date: ____________________

Signatures	Role
	Student
	Parent
	Administrator
	General Educator
	Special Educator
	Paraprofessional
	Mental Health Professional
	Other:
	Other:

What is a BIP?

Recall that a **BIP** is a behavior intervention plan written to address specific target behavior(s) and includes positive interventions, strategies, and supports. Much like the IEP, the BIP is written by a team made up of school faculty and parents who desire to see a student's behavior change. The behavior must be specifically named and is often called the **target behavior**. The BIP is used to encourage appropriate positive behaviors and to eliminate targeted negative behaviors.

Below is the first section of the BIP, which is the goal for the plan. The goal for the student must be measurable and observable.

Behavior Intervention Plan

Student: Brett Smith
School: Liberty Academic School
Date: 9/27/22

DOB: 3/24/07
Grade: 9th
Case Manager: Kelly Garman

Goal for Plan:
Brett will maintain safety 100% of the time across school settings during the first marking period (9/28/22–1/22/22) by accessing/utilizing strategies and supports for self-regulation during challenging moments.
Brett will complete 100% of classroom tasks with a compliance rate of 85% during the first marking period (9/28/22–1/22/22).

In many, if not most, circumstances, goals on a BIP are not set for the student to achieve 100% proficiency; however, in this case, the safety of all students and teachers is important. Everyone should be kept 100% safe 100% of the time; therefore, the goal for Brett is to maintain safe behavior all day every day. Additionally, the second goal for Brett is for him to complete all of his classroom tasks. For this goal, Brett is given a little bit of flexibility since his compliance rate is set at 85%. Clearly, it is hoped that he will exceed that expectation; but like all of us, Brett is not perfect, so we try to set him up for success by making his goal realistic and achievable.

The next section of the BIP is called Setting, Triggers, Contexts (Antecedents). In other words, we need to identify where the behavior occurs, what sets the behavior in motion, and what the circumstances are in which the target behaviors occur.

Setting Events, Triggers, Contexts (Antecedents):
Competitive games/activities
Unstructured social situations (i.e., Physical education (PE), recess, lunch, bus, transitions, bathroom)
Extended work periods (greater than 8–10 min)
Extended writing assignments
Idle wait time

Notice that information from the FBA is indicated in this section. The FBA noted that Brett oftentimes had difficulty in unstructured situations and during work periods lasting more than 10 min. The information in this section should be reflective of the evidence and information located in Brett's FBA.

The next section is called the **Hypothetical Function of Behaviors**. These are the assumptions made by the IEP team when considering all of the information and evidence on the FBA. This section identifies the hypothesis regarding the root causes of the behaviors. Recall that by determining the cause of the behavior, the plan is to use positive interventions and strategies to permanently eliminate or change the target behavior. Below you will find the hypothesized functions of the behaviors exhibited by Brett.

Hypothetical Function of Behaviors (per FBA 9/27/22):
To gain attention
To avoid/escape settings, tasks, individuals, or situations
To regulate affect

In some cases, Brett is described as seeking the attention of his peers for the purpose of developing friendships. His strategies oftentimes cause his classmates to avoid him. Additionally, Brett sometimes exhibits the target behaviors to avoid writing or waiting on others to "catch up" to him. Brett was also noted needing to move around and fidgeting. On this BIP, the IEP team is making an assumption regarding the motives for Brett's behaviors. These seem accurate, given the information that we currently have, but these may need to be revisited and revised if the target behaviors continue or escalate.

The next part of the plan includes the "action" items. The target behaviors are specifically addressed, and details are provided regarding the prevention of the behavior, the consequence of the behavior, and any follow-up. This information provides the "what to do" of the BIP.

Behavior Intervention Plan

Noncompliance	**Prevention:** • Agree on nonverbal cues between Brett and the teacher for self-advocacy when he needs or wants something • Provide access for typing when lengthier written work is required (more than one paragraph) • Schedule noncontingent breaks • Provide verbal checks to help him use time efficiently • Give motivators tied to task compliance and completion **Consequence:** • Give a direction • If student in noncompliant, repeat directions • If still noncompliant, repeat directions again and remind Brett of possible reinforcers if he complies • If still noncompliant, offer choices or alternatives and continue this process three times • After three attempts, give space and ignore as long as no safety issues arise • Attempt to reengage following next natural transition that occurs **Follow-up:** • Process all behaviors in a private, neutral setting once he has regained focus and calmed down • Utilize restorative questioning sheets to guide the discussion

Argumentative Behaviors	**Prevention:**
	• Avoid public correction
	• Create a safe space for Brett to retreat to without seeking permission to avoid engaging in argumentative behaviors
	• Record stressors
	• Monitor negative self-talk
	• Teach how to disagree appropriately
	    • "I" statements
	    • Draw it
	    • Write a complaint letter
	• Acknowledge his "power," but remind him no one is obligated to argue for him
	    • No one wins anything by arguing or giving in, but most of us argue and eventually give in
	    • Conflict motivators (rewards)
	    • Control/change your role in these moments
	• Praise his ambition and redirect to something more useful
	• Try to achieve mutual understanding
	Consequences:
	• Point out when Brett is arguing: "I feel like you are arguing with me. I need you to be flexible"
	• Encourage him to stop, stay calm, and make a new plan

<table>
<tr><td></td><td><ul>
<li>Use one of the following strategies:
<ul>
<li>"I statements"</li>
<li>Draw it</li>
<li>Write a letter of complaint</li>
</ul></li>
<li>If arguing continues, acknowledge Brett's "power," but remind him no one is obligated to argue with him. Use statements such as:
<ul>
<li>No one wins anything by arguing or giving in, but most of us argue and eventually give in. Think about what you want to control now. This conflict seems motivated by your opinions, interests, goals, desire to gain power, status, or something else. Let us discuss what you want or need</li>
</ul></li>
<li>Praise Brett's ambition and redirect to something more useful that would not embarrass him in front of his peers</li>
<li>Try to find mutual understanding</li>
</ul></td></tr>
</table>

<table>
<tr><td>Social Skills</td><td>Prevention:
<ul>
<li>Give a prompt regarding upcoming social skills requirements or situation that may cause him stress</li>
<li>Model expectations for group work</li>
<li>Allow Brett to observe activities prior to engaging</li>
<li>Try to explain the intention of others</li>
<li>Allow Brett to work independently unless someone is available to supervise the group</li>
<li>Use social skills scripts and social stories</li>
<li>Provide a limited number of social escape cards per day to allow Brett to leave an uncomfortable situation</li>
<li>Pair/group students strategically for success</li>
<li>Separate from triggering classmates</li>
</ul>
Consequences:
<ul>
<li>Review social stories</li>
<li>Role play or practice social skills needed in isolation with the school counselor or teacher</li>
<li>Repeat this as many times as possible to help solidify the skill</li>
</ul></td></tr>
</table>

<table>
<tr><td>Hyperactivity/
Impulsivity</td><td>Prevention:
<ul>
<li>Ignore rocking, bouncing, and fidgeting that does not interfere with learning</li>
<li>Provide extra space for Brett to move without touching or distracting others</li>
<li>Avoid unstructured time</li>
<li>Allowed structured exercise breaks every 20 min</li>
<li>Provide access to sensory tool kit</li>
<li>Consider allowing wiggle seat, fidget band on chair, and weighted lap pad during seat work</li>
<li>Display visual reminders of work area (boundary markers)</li>
</ul>
Consequences:
<ul>
<li>If hyperactive/impulsive behaviors are harmful, inconsiderate, or disrespectful, they should be addressed using restorative processing in a private setting to identify triggers and ways for Brett to manage his body and mind</li>
</ul></td></tr>
</table>

For this section, it is important for you to notice the details provided. This information is critical to eliminating or changing the target behaviors. Note that prevention is listed first. This is strategic. When problem behaviors can be prevented, they should be. This takes initiative from the teacher to be proactive. This can be a challenge when there are 20+ other students in the classroom, but it is important for the success of all learners. The rule is, when a target behavior can be prevented, try to prevent it. Despite being proactive, a target behavior is likely to occur, and when it does, the consequences noted on the BIP may help to deescalate the problem behavior or to redirect the student. Note that the consequences are designed to continue to train the student to learn how to manage his own behavior. This is an important component of the BIP. When students manage their own behavior, there is more time for teaching and learning.

In the next section, you will see that specific interventions are put into place and the specific person(s) responsible for the action item is noted. This is the "plan." Read this section carefully and take note of the specific items mentioned that will be implemented to positively support Brett so that his target behaviors can be eliminated or changed.

Interventions:	**Person(s) Responsible for Implementing Intervention:**

• **Check-in/Check-out (Social-Emotional)**
  ◦ Check-in with classroom teacher in the morning
  ◦ Check-outs with homeroom teacher before leaving, including reflection on positive behavior and goals sent home daily
  ◦ Breaks requested throughout the day
	• **Check-in/Check-out (Social-Emotional)**
	  ◦ School social worker/psychologist, special educator, general education teacher

• **Social Skills Training**
  ◦ Access to and review of social stories
  ◦ Planned, noncompetitive recess opportunities
  ◦ Access to appropriate coping strategies
	• **Social Skills Training**
	  ◦ School social worker/psychologist to provide stories, help with development of recess activities, develop coping strategies
	  ◦ Teacher will assist with access and encouragement

• **Classroom Accommodations**
  ◦ Access to bulleted list outlining expectations for each of his daily activities
  ◦ Preset verbal expectations in "I need you to…" rather than, "do not…"
  ◦ Access to coping strategies and tools
  ◦ Preferential seating
  ◦ Utilization of appropriate preventative and consequence techniques including referral when necessary
  ◦ Proximity to teacher
  ◦ Graphic organizers
  ◦ Assignments broken down into smaller more manageable sizes
  ◦ Check to ensure understanding of assignments
  ◦ Oral discussion with teacher before writing assignment
  ◦ Small group testing
	• **Classroom Accommodations**
	  ◦ Teacher and special educator

• **Daily Report Card/Token Economy**
  • Earned independent time and rewards for completing tasks and maintaining safety
  • Point system to communicate daily behaviors with family
  • Reflection on positive behaviors and goals for the next day
	• **Daily Report Card/Token Economy**
	  • Teachers will assign points throughout the day
	  • Special educator/homeroom teacher will assist with positive reflection and goal for the next day
	  • Rewards will be based on what student earns but may include mental health personnel, principal, assistant principal, teachers, or parents

• **Identification of Trusted Adult in Each Setting**	• **Identification of Trusted Adult in Each Setting** • Teachers

The final section of the BIP is simple the date the BIP was reviewed and the signatures. Not all of the signatures will be needed, but all relevant signatures should be included for accountability purposes.

Review Date: ____________________

Signatures	Role
	Student
	Parent
	Administrator
	General Educator
	Special Educator
	LEA
	Paraprofessional
	Mental Health Professional
	Other:
	Other:

Chapter Highlights

A Functional Behavior Assessment (FBA) is an assessment of target behavior(s) and requires information and evidence to determine the cause or purpose of a behavior.

The FBA information and evidence are utilized by the IEP team to write a BIP to help eliminate or change the behavior.

The BIP should include positive strategies, interventions, and supports to address the target behaviors.

Information collected during the FBA should be used to determine the BIP.

Recall that the goal of the BIP is to determine the root cause of the behavior in an effort to permanently eliminate or change target behaviors.

Hypothetical Function of Behaviors are the assumptions made by the IEP team based on hypothetical situations when considering all of the information and evidence on the FBA.

Chapter Review Questions

1. Write the definition of a Behavioral Intervention Plan.
2. Write three goals for a BIP for a student who has high functioning autism. Include the age/grade level.
3. Describe the setting events, triggers, and context for three target behaviors.
4. Determine a hypothetical function of behaviors for a student. Provide all necessary details to make the determination.
5. Write preventions, consequences, and follow-ups for a target behavior of your choice.
6. Describe interventions and persons responsible for implementation for the target behaviors above.

IEP: Documents & Details Essential for a Quality Individual Education Program

Liberty Academic School

Documents & Details Essential for a Quality Individual Education Program

Liberty Academic School
XXXX XXXX XXXXXX
XXXXXXX XXXXXX
XXXXXXX XXXXXX
Telephone: XXXXXX
Fax: XXXXXXXXXX
Email: xxxxx@xxxx.com
Website: www.xxxxxxx.com

Individualized Education Plan
Meeting Notice

Name: David and Mary Smith   Date: September 7, 2022

You are invited to attend an IEP meeting for your child: Brett Smith

Meeting Details:

Date: 9/20/22

Time: 1:30

Location: D221

Purpose of Meeting:

______ IEP Development
__✓__ IEP Review
______ Discuss Services[1]
__✓__ Transition[2]
______ Manifestation Determination
______ Other

[1]If the purpose of this meeting is to discuss services, service personnel may be invited.

[2]If the purpose of the meeting is to discuss transition, the student will be invited.

If you are unable to attend the meeting at this scheduled time and location, or if you would like additional information prior to the meeting, please contact the IEP team leader below to reschedule.

Kelly Garman	Kgarman@email.com	(111)-111-1111
Team Leader	Email	Phone Number

Participants Involved:
Below is a list of participants invited to this IEP meeting. Attendance is required.

Name of Participant	Position
David & Mary Smith	Father and Mother
Brett Smith	Student
Shonda Miller	Administrator
Kelly Garman	Special Education Teacher, Team Leader
Stuart Fisher	General Education Teacher
Dr. Nathaniel Salinas	Guidance Counselor
Russ Greer	Speech/Language Therapist

Individualized Education Plan
Meeting Notice, continued

Please keep the first page, and return this page to the team leader.

Kelly Garman	Kgarman@email.com	(111)-111-1111
Team Leader	Email	Phone Number

Meeting Details:

Date: 9/20/22

Time: 1:30

Location: D221

Based on the date and location above:

__✓__ I WILL attend the IEP meeting as scheduled

_____ I WILL NOT attend the IEP meeting as scheduled

If you will not attend the meeting. Please complete the following:

_____ Please contact me to reschedule the meeting.

_____ I can participate via WebEx or ________________

_____ Please hold the meeting without me.

_____ I give permission to proceed without a meeting.

_____ If no response, proceed with meeting.

_____ I would like to share my input via other means (email, telephone, mail).

David Smith
Signature of Parent

9/10/22
Date

Liberty Academic School

XXXX XXXX XXXXXX

XXXXXXX XXXXXX

XXXXXXX XXXXXX

Telephone: XXXXXX

Fax: XXXXXXXXXX

Email: xxxxx@xxxx.com

Website: www.xxxxxxx.com

Individualized Education Plan

Team Member Excusal Request

If the team member's area of curriculum, related services, or expertise will be discussed, the team member may be excused, but must provide written comments and submit for approval 10 days prior to the meeting. If the team members' area of curriculum, related services, or expertise will not be discussed the team member may be excused without written documentation.

The following team members have requested to be excused from the meeting.

Name of Participant	Position	Reason
Russ Greer	Speech/Language Therapist	Mr. Greer is having surgery on this date and requests to be updated with Brett's needs and will accommodate his speech schedule as needed.

The excusal request is for the following date:

Student Name: Brett Smith

IEP Meeting Date: September 20, 2022

Meeting Location: D221

✓ **I agree to excuse the above team member from the meeting.**

David Smith
Signature of Parent

9/10/22
Date

Shonda Miller
Signature of Administrator/District Representative

September 10, 2022
Date

Liberty Academic School
XXXX XXXX XXXXXX
XXXXXXX XXXXXX
XXXXXXX XXXXXX
Telephone: XXXXXX
Fax: XXXXXXXXXX
Email: xxxxx@xxxx.com
Website: www.xxxxxxx.com

Individualized Education Plan
Cover Page

Student Name: Brett Smith Date: 9/20/22

Disability: Specific Learning Disability and Attention Deficit Hyperactivity Disorder

Grade: 9 DOB: 3/24/07 Age: 15

Parent/Guardian Name: David & Mary Smith

Street Address: 1101 First Street

City: Majestic State: VA Zip Code: 12345

Phone #: (123)456-7890

A copy of the IEP was given to the parent/guardian/student by: Kelly Garman

IEP Team Leader: Kelly Garman Phone #: (111)-111-1111

The Individualized Education Plan (IEP) that accompanies this document is meant to support the positive process and team approach. The IEP is a working document that outlines the vision for the student's future and includes the student's strengths and needs.

IEP Summary Information	
Projected IEP Start Date:	9/30/22
Projected IEP End Date:	6/24/23
Projected Annual Review Date:	6/24/23
Projected Date for Reevaluation:	6/24/25
Extended School Services	No
Behavior Intervention Plan	Yes
Supplementary Aids and Services	Yes
Assistive Technology	No
Supports for School Personnel	No
Testing Accommodations	Yes
Participate in State/District Assessments	Yes
Special Transportation	No

Participants Involved

The list below indicates that the individual participated in the development of the IEP and the decisions regarding placement. Participation does not authorize consent. Parent consent (or student if 18+ years of age) is indicated on the "Prior Notice" page.

Name of Participant	Position
David & Mary Smith	Father and Mother
Brett Smith	Student
Shonda Miller	Administrator
Kelly Garman	Special Education Teacher, Team Leader
Stuart Fisher	General Education Teacher
Dr. Nathaniel Salinas	Guidance Counselor
Russ Greer	Speech/Language Therapist

Liberty Academic School
XXXX XXXX XXXXXX
XXXXXXX XXXXXX
XXXXXXX XXXXXX
Telephone: XXXXXX
Fax: XXXXXXXXXX
Email: xxxxx@xxxx.com
Website: www.xxxxxxx.com

Individualized Education Plan
Summary of Performance
Factors for IEP Team Consideration

Student Name: Brett Smith Date: 9/7/22

Disability: Specific Learning Disability and Attention Deficit Hyperactivity Disorder

DOB: 3/24/07 Age: 15 Grade: 9

IEP Team Manager: Kelly Garman

The following information should be considered by the IEP team in regards to educational decisions made for the student, as it serves as a summary of the student's performance. Please see other sections of the IEP, as noted, for more precise details concerning specific areas of learning for this student.

1. Summary of Academic Achievement:

Include results of the initial or most recent evaluation of this student.

Cognitive testing indicates overall cognitive functioning in the borderline range with a Full-Scale IQ of 73 SS. Verbal Comprehension (73 SS) skills increased from the previous evaluation (65 SS) and is in the borderline range, along with Perceptual Reasoning (78 SS).

Mathematics

Numerical Operations (72 SS) is in the borderline range. Significant deficits are noted in math Problem-Solving (59 SS). Inconsistent focused attention was noted during testing. For example, Brett was redirected three times based on lack of answering questions while looking away from the test and tapping his pencil. Additionally, Brett asked to get water twice and to stand up to work once. Brett's core math skills are significantly below grade level.

In the resource classroom, he struggles with equations, computation, and multistep word problems.

Reading/Written Language

Speech and language reevaluation reveals a Core Language score (76 SS) in the borderline range; however, significant improvement is noted from previous test score (61SS). During his twice-weekly 30-min speech/language therapy sessions, Brett exhibits effort on a mostly consistent basis. The speech/language pathologist noted improvements in verbal comprehension based on test scores 73 (SS) and improved participation based on teacher observation. Brett continues to work on soliciting additional info or asking for repetition when unsure.

Reading comprehension skills (94 SS) and decoding skills (93 SS) are in the average range. He can decode and answer basic comprehension questions. Long-term retention of material is an area of concern. Word reading (75 SS) is in the borderline range. Significant deficits are noted in listening comprehension (60 SS). Effort was inconsistent during testing. For example, Brett asked random off-topic questions and was redirected by the teacher twice.

Additionally, shortly after Brett began reading the third section of the reading comprehension section, he put his head down on the desk to take a break twice.

In the resource room, Brett consistently uses reading strategies and refers back to the text to assist with comprehension. Assistance is required with higher-order thinking skills. A graphic organizer is used for writing grammar. Mechanics are weak based on writing samples (documents included in the IEP as evidence).

2. Strengths of the student:

Brett is highly motivated and gets along well with others. Though he benefits from working in a small group setting for his academics, he also enjoys social interaction in a large group setting. Brett is also motivated by information pertaining to automobiles.

3. Summary of Functional Performance, as applicable:

Behavior scales indicate a few conduct issues. Progress is hindered by lack of attention and concentration. Brett demonstrates weak organizational skills and does not complete assignments and homework in a timely manner. He requires consistent teacher support to accomplish his work accurately and in a timely manner. His parents indicate that Brett is on medication for Attention Deficit Hyperactivity Disorder (ADHD) and for tics. Stress increases his tics.

4. Summary of Transition: Postsecondary Goals, as applicable:

According to his parents, David and Mary, Brett's interests are in video games, cars, and sports (soccer, football, basketball) but his desire is to become an auto mechanic.

Career Cluster Interest Survey reveals career interests in the areas of Information Technology, Science/Technology/Engineering, and Marketing. CITE Learning Styles Instrument indicate five areas of major learning preference: Auditory/Numerical, Auditory/Language, Auditory/Visual/Kinesthetic, Social/Group, and Expressive/Oral.

5. Parental concerns for enhancing the student's education:

David and Mary are concerned that Brett's math skills may hinder him from achieving his post-secondary goals. Although he has made some progress for the past few years, they want him to be on track to finish high school on grade level in math, as well as in all academic areas.

6. Communication needs of the student:

Brett continues to work on asking for additional help when he needs further clarification on a concept or problem. He needs to be a stronger self-advocate when it comes to asking for assistance. He is working on this skill with his speech/language pathologist.

7. Need for benchmarks or short-term objectives:

Brett needs to be assessed quarterly in the content areas in order to measure progress. He will take the state end-of-subject and/or end-of-grade tests and local benchmark tests at regular intervals along with grade-level peers with appropriate accommodations to measure his progress against state and local standards. He also needs to have measurable short-term objectives for reading, writing, and math.

8. Does the student require an Assistive Technology device and/or service?

Yes or No (circle one)

If yes, does the committee recommend the device(s) be used in the student's home?

Yes or No (circle one)

9. Does the student need strategies, including behavioral interventions, supports, and other strategies to address behaviors that impede the student's learning or that of others?

Yes or No (circle one)

If yes, does the student need a behavioral intervention plan?

Yes or No (circle one)

10. In the case of a student with limited English proficiency, does he/she need special education services to address his/her language needs as they relate to the IEP?

Yes or No or Not Applicable (circle one)

11. In the case of a student who is blind or is visually impaired, the IEP team must provide for instruction or use of Braille if assessment results indicate need. When considering that Braille is not appropriate for the child, the IEP team may use the Functional Vision and Learning Media Assessment for Students who are Pre-Academic or Academic and Visually Impaired in Grades K-12 (FVLMA) or similar instrument;

Does this student need instruction in Braille or use of Braille?

Yes or No or Not Applicable (circle one)

12. In the case of a student who is deaf or hard of hearing, consider the student's language and communication needs, opportunities for direct communications with peers and professional personnel in the student's language and communication mode, academic level, and full range of needs, including opportunities for direct instruction in the student's language and communication mode.

Does this student need a particular device or service to address his/her communication needs?

Yes or No or Not Applicable (circle one)

13. Extended School Year (ESY)

Does this student require extended school year services?

Yes or No (circle one)

Liberty Academic School
XXXX XXXX XXXXXX
XXXXXXX XXXXXX
XXXXXXX XXXXXX
Telephone: XXXXXX
Fax: XXXXXXXXXX
Email: xxxxx@xxxx.com
Website: www.xxxxxxx.com

Individualized Education Plan
Present Level of Academic Achievement and Functional Performance (PLAAFP)

Student Name: Brett Smith Meeting Date: 9/20/22

Student Strengths, Preferences, and Interests:

- Brett's strength is that he is motivated to learn and helpful to the teacher and his peers.
- His interests are in video games, cars, and sports (soccer, football, basketball). He will occasionally check out a book from the library on hot rod cars or how to build engines.
- According to the CITE Learning Styles Instrument, Brett prefers five areas of major learning: Auditory/Numerical, Auditory/Language, Auditory/Visual/Kinesthetic, Social/Group, and Expressive/Oral.
- Cluster Interest Survey reveals career interests in the areas of Information Technology, Science/Technology/Engineering, and Marketing.

Assessment/Evaluation Data:

Evaluation/Reports Included:

Parent Report and Observations (01/31/21)
Speech/Language Re-evaluation (01//11/21)
Speech/Language Progress Summary (01/15/2021)
Guidance Report (01/31/21)
Teacher Progress Summary (01/31/21)
Educational Evaluation (01/12/21)

Test Results:

WIAT—III (01/12/21)
Basic Reading 84 (Standard Score), 14 (Percentile Rank)
Essay Comp: Grammar & Mechanics 82 (SS), 10 (PR)
Essay Composition 77 (SS), 5 (PR)
Expressive Vocabulary 74 (SS), 4 (PR)
Listening Comprehension 60 (SS), 0.3 (PR)
Oral Discourse Comprehension 56 (SS), 0.2 (PR)
Oral Expression 87 (SS), 19 (PR)

Oral Language 70 (SS), 2 (PR)
Oral Reading Accuracy 75 (SS), 5 (PR)
Oral Reading Fluency 82 (SS), 13 (PR)
Oral Reading Rate 84 (SS), 14 (PR)
Oral Word Fluency 96 (SS), 38 (PR)

Reading Comprehension 93 (SS), 32 (PR)
Receptive Vocabulary 92 (SS), 3 (PR)
Sentence Building 74 (SS), 4 (PR)
Sentence Combining 84 (SS), 14 (PR)
Sentence Composition 78 (SS), 7 (PR)
Sentence Repetition 100 (SS), 50 (PR)
Spelling 80 (SS), 9 (PR)
Theme Development and Text Organization 67 (SS), 1 (PR)
Total Achievement 71 (SS), 3 (PR)
Total Reading 82 (SS), 12 (PR)
Word Count 89 (SS), 23 (PR)
Word Reading 75 (SS), 5 (PR)
Written Expression 74 (SS), 4 (PR)
Math Fluency—Addition 83 (SS), 14 (PR)
Math Fluency—Subtraction 86 (SS), 18 (PR)
Math Fluency—Multiplication 71 (SS), 3 (PR)
Math Problem Solving 60 (SS), 0.4 (PR)
Mathematics 66 (SS), 1 (PR)
Numerical Operations 72 (SS), 3 (PR)
Math Fluency 78 (SS), 7 (PR)

Wechsler Abbreviated Scale of Intelligence-II
Full-Scale IQ 73 (SS), 5 (PR)
Perceptual Reasoning 78 (SS), 7 (PR)
Verbal Comprehension 73 (SS), 4 (PR)

CELF-5
Core Language Score 76 (SS), 5 (PR)
Formulated Sentences 6 (SS), 9 (PR)
Recalling Sentences 8 (SS), 25 (PR)
Semantic Relationships 5 (SS), 5 (PR)
Understanding Spoken Paragraphs 5 (SS), 5 (PR)

State and District-wide Assessments:
None

Current Student Academic Performance:

Writing:
Brett's writing skills are progressing slowly. The writing process is hindered by his lack of ability to maintain focus. He can generate ideas for writing, but he needs assistance to include sufficient details. Graphic organizers and outlines support his writing, and one must still be provided for him in most instances. Essays pose a significant problem for Brett due to the number of organizational elements required for success. His grammar and mechanics skills are below grade level. When prompted to write about a topic related to his required reading, such as a book report or essay, Brett struggles due to reading comprehension difficulties and his ability to organize his thoughts into a coherent essay.

Reading:
Brett is able to answer basic knowledge questions when reading at his independent level. He has difficulty with questions that require higher-order thinking skills, context clues, and determining the meaning of unfamiliar words. He also struggles with drawing conclusions and making inferences, which negatively impacts his comprehension and retention when reading from grade-level textbooks. Specific reading strategies

such as re-reading the text, self-question, and summarizing his understanding of the text have helped, but he is hesitant to use these strategies unless prompted. He does not independently use details to answer questions accurately and to support his inferences and ideas. At times, his inability to stay focused impacts his ability to understand and retain information.

Speech/Language:
Brett is a considerate, respectful, and typically engaged student. His attention issues present a challenge quite often, but he responds when redirected. Brett is able to participate in conversational dialogue, but he is negatively impacted by language processing and auditory memory problems. He frequently demonstrates difficulty with higher-order questions and organizing sentences when incorporating abstract ideas, but is able to use basic communication skills. Brett has been working on strategies to improve his word retrieval and auditory memory skills, but he continues to struggle. Brett's articulation is characterized by a distortion of the /p/ phoneme in many positions of words and blends.

Math:
When he is feeling confident, Brett works diligently to complete his assignments. However, he benefits from constant support and reinforcement as well as the use of a calculator. He has difficulty learning grade-level math concepts, and he is most successful in a small group or one-to-one setting. He can follow one-step procedures, but he has difficulty with multiple-step problems and simple computation. Even after extensive modeling and guided practice, Brett requires support to accurately follow mathematical procedures and solve problems. He also has a hard time remembering and applying concepts over time, which makes cumulative math exams extremely challenging.

Effects of Disability on General Curriculum:

Describe the effect of student needs on progress in the general curriculum or, for a preschool student, effect of student needs on participation in appropriate activities.

Writing:
Brett needs to include sufficient details in his writing to support ideas and inferences and utilize a standard format to organize required elements of an essay. Proofreading and checking his writing for grammar and mechanics need to be a consistent part of his writing routine.

Reading:
Brett needs to develop his comprehension of content material. He needs to develop his ability to answer questions requiring higher-order thinking skills. He needs to use context clues to determine the meaning of unknown words.

Speech/Language:
Brett needs to develop language processing, verbal/written expression, auditory memory, and word retrieval skills. Therapist support is needed in order to monitor his articulation of the /p/ phoneme in structured speech and spontaneous conversation.

Math:
Brett needs to improve his recall of basic facts and accuracy of computation. He requires direct support to learn and practice grade-level math skills. He struggles with multistep procedures. A list of steps to follow from the beginning of a problem until the end increases his ability to succeed.

Summary:
Brett has a significant delay in written expression, language skills, speech skills, attention skills, math calculation, and math concepts which interferes with age-appropriate activities in the general education curriculum.

Current Student Functional Performance:

Social Competence:

Brett is helpful, cooperative, and friendly, which are skills that strengthen his social competence. His social and emotional levels are within age expectations. At times, Brett is quiet and withdrawn; this typically occurs when he is feeling stressed or lacking confidence in his ability. There are no social or emotional needs that require special education services at this time.

Physical Development:

Brett enjoys sports and participates in Physical Education class. Brett's diagnosed medical condition impacts his education. He is diagnosed with ADHD, Dysgraphia, and Transient Tic Disorder (involuntary tics). He exhibits symptoms of cognitive impulsivity, distractibility, and inattention. David, Brett's father, reports that Brett is exhausted from the school day and finds it exceptionally challenging for him to complete homework or study after school. He is on medication for ADHD and Transient Tic Disorder.

Needs: Brett needs to continue to learn compensatory skills for the negative educational impact of his diagnosed ADHD.

Based on Effects, Describe Deficits that Require Functional Support:

Brett needs a teacher-to-student ratio that is small. He needs frequent redirection to attend to tasks. Seating near the front of the room will minimize distractions and sitting near the teacher will allow for frequent redirection and opportunities to check-in. Information should be taught sequentially with clear steps. He needs repetition and review of lessons as well as assistance with organizational skills and time management. He also craves social interaction, which may impact the least restrictive environment (LRE).

Liberty Academic School
XXXX XXXX XXXXXX
XXXXXXX XXXXXX
XXXXXXX XXXXXX
Telephone: XXXXXX
Fax: XXXXXXXXXX
Email: xxxxx@xxxx.com
Website: www.xxxxxxx.com

Individualized Education Plan
Measurable Annual Goals

Student Name: Brett Smith   Meeting Date: 9/20/22

The following goals are recommended to enable the student to be involved in and progress in the general education curriculum, address other educational needs that result from the student's disability, and prepare the student to meet his or her post-high-school goals.

Annual Goal: One		
Goal: Reading In 12 months, Brett will read and exhibit comprehension of the ninth grade text, including prose, drama, poetry, and content area subject text in 80% of given opportunities, as measured biweekly on teacher-devised tests or text worksheets.		
Standard of learning related to this goal: Virginia Standard 9.4 The student will read, comprehend, and analyze a variety of literacy texts including narratives, narrative nonfiction, poetry, and drama.		
Progress toward this goal will be measured: (Check all that apply)		
✓ Tests and Quizzes __ Standardized Test __ Norm Referenced Test __ Other Assessment	✓ Classwork __ Projects __ Homework ✓ Participation	__ Written Report ✓ Observation __ Checklist __ Other
Progress toward this goal will be reported:		
Biweekly		
Short-Term Objectives or Benchmarks, if necessary: or circle if N/A		
Objective/Benchmark One: Given a literacy text, Brell will read aloud and explain the author's main idea and purpose in a writing sample, based on a rubric, in three out of four trials by December 13, 2022. Assessment method: Teacher observation and writing rubric		
Objective/Benchmark Two: Given a literary text, Brett will define the relationships between and among elements of literature: characters, plot, setting, tone, point of view, and theme in three out of four trails by March 13, 2023. Assessment method: Writing elements rubric		

Objective/Benchmark Three:
Given a literary text, Brett will analyze how an author's specific word choices and syntax achieve special effects and support the author's purpose. The literary text will be read, and Brett will correctly answer 80% of the questions pertaining to the text in three out of four trials as graded by end of novel test.

Assessment method: *End of novel test*

Annual Goal: Two

Goal: *Reading*
In 12 months, when presented with narrative or specific informational text, Brett will accurately answer questions that require higher-order thinking skills (making predictions and inferences, drawing conclusions, making judgments, supporting views, and applying knowledge in new ways) in 80% of given opportunities, as measured biweekly on teacher-devised tests or text worksheets.

Standard of learning related to this goal: *Virginia Standard 9.4*
l) Make predictions, inferences, draw conclusions, and connect prior knowledge to support reading comprehension.

Progress toward this goal will be measured: (Check all that apply)

✓ Tests and Quizzes	✓ Classwork	___ Written Report
___ Standardized Test	___ Projects	___ Observation
___ Norm-Referenced Test	___ Homework	___ Checklist
___ Other Assessment	___ Participation	___ Other

Progress toward this goal will be reported:

Biweekly

Short-Term Objectives or Benchmarks, if necessary: or circle if N/A

Objective/Benchmark One:
When given a grade-level textbook narrative, Brett will answer comprehension questions following the narrative that require making judgments and presenting supporting evidence with 80% accuracy.

Assessment method: *Teacher graded comprehension questions (classwork)*

Objective/Benchmark Two:
When given a grade-level textbook narrative, Brett will make predictions based on the narrative with 80% accuracy on curriculum based assessment.

Assessment method: *Curriculum-based assessment*

Objective/Benchmark Three:

Assessment method:

Annual Goal: Three

Goal: Reading
In 12 months, when presented with informational text from content area subjects, Brett will use strategies of re-reading material, using context clues to help define words within the text, visualizing, and summarizing to assist in answering questions about the text that test for understanding in 80% of given opportunities, as measured biweekly on teacher-devised tests or text worksheets.

Standard of learning related to this goal: Virginia Standard 9.3b and 9.4m
9.3b) Use context, structure, and connotations to determine meanings of words and phrases.
9.4m) Use reading strategies to monitor comprehension throughout the reading process.

Progress toward this goal will be measured: (Check all that apply)

✓ Tests and Quizzes	✓ Classwork	___ Written Report
___ Standardized Test	___ Projects	___ Observation
___ Norm Referenced Test	___ Homework	___ Checklist
___ Other Assessment	___ Participation	___ Other

Progress toward this goal will be reported:

Biweekly

Short-Term Objectives or Benchmarks, if necessary: or circle if N/A

Objective/Benchmark One: After being given instruction on starting and maintaining a vocabulary word journal, Brett will generate his own vocabulary word journal and enter new/unfamiliar words from his reading materials/assignments. Within his journal, Brett will write each word, a dictionary definition or his own definition for each word, and a sentence that uses each word. The words will be spelled correctly, definitions will be accurate, and sentences will have the words used correctly for at least 70% of his entries.

Assessment method: Teacher review of journal entries

Objective/Benchmark Two: Given a worksheet that has several short passages, Brett will define new words that are in the passages based on the context in which those words are used. Brett will also write short summaries of the passages. Both the definitions and summaries will be correct/accurate with at least 70% accuracy.

Assessment method: Worksheets

Objective/Benchmark Three: In 10 weeks, Brett will be able to correctly define words and phrases in textbooks based on the context, structure, and connotations of how those words and phrases are used with at least 70% accuracy. Additionally, Brett will summarize the contents of those passages and answer comprehension questions related to those passages, and he will answer with at least 70% accuracy.

Assessment method: Test

<table>
<tr><th colspan="3">Annual Goal: Four</th></tr>
<tr><td colspan="3">Goal: Writing
In 12 months, Brett will write narrative, expository, and persuasive writings with relevant content to develop complex ideas, including transitions to clarify ideas and precise and domain-specific vocabulary, written in formal style using an objective tone, as measured biweekly on teacher-devised tests or text worksheets with 80% accuracy.</td></tr>
<tr><td colspan="3">Standard of learning related to this goal: Virginia standard 9.6
The student will develop narrative, expository, and persuasive writings for a variety of audiences and purposes.</td></tr>
<tr><td colspan="3">Progress toward this goal will be measured: (Check all that apply)</td></tr>
<tr><td>✓ Tests and Quizzes
___ Standardized Test
___ Norm Referenced Test
___ Other Assessment</td><td>✓ Classwork
___ Projects
___ Homework
___ Participation</td><td>✓ Written Report
___ Observation
___ Checklist
___ Other</td></tr>
<tr><td colspan="3">Progress toward this goal will be reported:</td></tr>
<tr><td colspan="3">Biweekly</td></tr>
<tr><td colspan="3">Short-Term Objectives or Benchmarks, if necessary: or circle if N/A</td></tr>
<tr><td colspan="3">Objective/Benchmark One:
Given a writing prompt from different genres of literature, Brett will write five topic sentences with at least 80% accuracy.

Assessment method: Writing rubric</td></tr>
<tr><td colspan="3">Objective/Benchmark Two:
Brett will produce a writing sample with a thesis statement for each of several different given topics, and he will write a thesis statement, topic sentences, and an outline for one topic of his choice with 80% accuracy as determined by writing rubric.

Assessment method: Writing rubric</td></tr>
<tr><td colspan="3">Objective/Benchmark Three:
In 10 weeks, Brett will be able to identify thesis statements and topic sentences in 7 out of 10 questions on a test, and he will write three to five clear and concise paragraphs on the topic he chose from his earlier assignment (from Objective/Benchmark Two above) with at least 70% accuracy.

Assessment method: Test</td></tr>
</table>

Annual Goal: Five		
Goal: *Mathematics* *In 12 months, when presented with a variety of grade-level multistep linear and quadratic equations, Brett will identify each step and complete them in the correct logical sequential order, as measured biweekly by curriculum-based worksheets and assessments 80% of the time.*		
Standard of learning related to this goal: *Virginia standard A.4* *The student will solve multistep linear and quadratic equations with two variables.*		
Progress toward this goal will be measured: (Check all that apply)		
✓ Tests and Quizzes ___ Standardized Test ___ Norm Referenced Test ___ Other Assessment	✓ Classwork ___ Projects ___ Homework ___ Participation	___ Written Report ___ Observation ___ Checklist ___ Other
Progress toward this goal will be reported:		
Biweekly		
Short-Term Objectives or Benchmarks, if necessary: or circle if N/A		
Objective/Benchmark One: *In 12 weeks, when presented with 10 multistep linear and quadratic equations for a given variable, Brett will follow the correct logical sequential order to correctly solve the equations with at least 50% accuracy.* Assessment method: *Curriculum-based worksheets and assessments*		
Objective/Benchmark Two: *In 24 weeks, when presented with 10 multistep linear and quadratic equations for a given variable, Brett will follow the correct logical sequential order, without teacher support, to correctly solve the equations with at least 80% accuracy.* Assessment method: *Curriculum-based worksheets and assessments*		
Objective/Benchmark Three: Assessment method:		

Annual Goal: Six		
Goal: *Speaking/Listening* *In 12 months, Brett will make inferences and draw conclusions in writing and verbally on a written text or other variety of media, read aloud to him as measured biweekly by recorded observations and/or standardized tests with 80% accuracy.*		
Standard of learning related to this goal: *Virginia Standard 9.2* *The student will produce, analyze, and evaluate auditory, visual, and written media messages.*		
Progress toward this goal will be measured: (Check all that apply)		
___ Tests and Quizzes ___ Standardized Test ___ Norm-Referenced Test ___ Other Assessment	✓ Classwork ___ Projects ___ Homework ✓ Participation	✓ Written Report ✓ Observation ___ Checklist ___ Other
Progress toward this goal will be reported:		
Biweekly		
Short-Term Objectives or Benchmarks, if necessary: or circle if N/A		
Objective/Benchmark One: *Brett will make inferences and draw conclusions based on the text read aloud to him and correctly answer 8 out of 10 questions on a curriculum based assessment.* Assessment method: *Curriculum-based assessment*		
Objective/Benchmark Two: *Brett will analyze and evaluate a video presentation of a poem delivered via the internet by writing a paragraph drawing accurate conclusions based on the poem as determined by teacher-made rubric with 80% accuracy.* Assessment method: *Teacher graded assignment using rubric*		
Objective/Benchmark Three: Assessment method:		

Annual Goal: Seven		
Goal: *Speech/Language* *In 12 months, Brett will monitor and produce the /p/ phoneme in all positions of words and in conversational speech, as measured biweekly by recorded observations and/or tests, with 80% accuracy.*		
Standard of learning related to this goal: *Virginia Standard 9.1d* *9.1d) Use grammatically correct language, including vocabulary appropriate to the topic, audience, and purpose.*		
Progress toward this goal will be measured: (Check all that apply)		
✓ Tests and Quizzes ___ Standardized Test ___ Norm-Referenced Test ___ Other Assessment	✓ Classwork ___ Projects ___ Homework ✓ Participation	___ Written Report ✓ Observation ___ Checklist ___ Other
Progress toward this goal will be reported:		
Biweekly		
Short-Term Objectives or Benchmarks, if necessary: or circle if N/A		
Objective/Benchmark One: *Given a topic, Brett will produce grammatically correct language, including the /p/ phoneme, in a written short story with 80% accuracy. He will monitor and self-correct the paper. The final version will be submitted to fulfill the 80% accuracy requirement.* Assessment method: *Self-monitoring/correcting and teacher-graded submission*		
Objective/Benchmark Two: *Given a topic, Brett will produce grammatically correct language, including the /p/ phoneme, in a short story, as presented aloud to the teacher, with 80% accuracy, as determined by participation and teacher observation.* Assessment method: *Participation and teacher observation*		
Objective/Benchmark Three: Assessment method:		

Annual Goal: Eight		
Goal: *Speech/Language* *In 12 months, Brett will use retrieval strategies, as measured biweekly by recorded observations and/or standardized tests, with 80% accuracy.*		
Standard of learning related to this goal: *Virginia standard 9.1f and 9.1h* *f) Use verbal and nonverbal techniques for presentation.* *h) Give impromptu responses to questions about presentations.*		
Progress toward this goal will be measured: (Check all that apply)		
___ Tests and Quizzes _X_ Standardized Test ___ Norm-Referenced Test ___ Other Assessment	___ Classwork ___ Projects ___ Homework ___ Participation	___ Written Report _X_ Observation ___ Checklist ___ Other
Progress toward this goal will be reported:		
Biweekly		
Short-Term Objectives or Benchmarks, if necessary: or circle if N/A		
Objective/Benchmark One: *After a classroom presentation, Brett will answer orally delivered content questions related to the presentation, as given by the teacher. He will use retrieval strategies to answer the questions with 80% accuracy as determined by teacher observation.* Assessment method: *Teacher observation*		
Objective/Benchmark Two: *Given a standardized test, Brett will score 80% accuracy in the language sections requiring retrieval strategies as determined by standardized test and teacher observation.* Assessment method: *Standardized test and teacher observation*		
Objective/Benchmark Three: Assessment method:		
Reporting Progress:		
*Progress will be reported at least as often as students without disabilities. Identify when periodic reports on the student's progress toward meeting the annual goals will be provided to the student's parents: *There will be four written progress reports during the school year.* *For the purposes of evaluating/assessing the student's progress on goals, assessment methods may include testing, benchmark assessment, curriculum-based assessment, and clinical observation.*		

Liberty Academic School
XXXX XXXX XXXXXX
XXXXXXX XXXXXX
XXXXXXX XXXXXX
Telephone: XXXXXX
Fax: XXXXXXXXXX
Email: xxxxx@xxxx.com
Website: www.xxxxxxx.com

Individualized Education Plan
Least Restrictive Environment
Accommodations/Modifications

Student Name: Brett Smith Meeting Date: 9/20/21

This student will be provided access to the general education, special education, other school services and activities, and education-related settings:

______ With no accommodations/modifications

__✓__ With accommodations/modifications as follows:

Accommodations/Modifications					
Accommodations/ Modifications	Delivery Recommendations	Least Restrictive Environment	Frequency	Duration	Services Begin
Tests and assignments read aloud to student	As needed	Special education classroom	Daily	During instructional class time or during tests	9/23/22
Support for organizational skills	Agenda checked daily by teacher at end of class	Special and general education classroom	Conclusion of every class	Throughout the school day	9/23/22
Refocusing and redirection	Brett requires assistance in attending to classroom activities	Special and general education classroom	Daily	Throughout the school day	9/23/22
Strategic Seating	Brett focuses best when placed in close proximity to the teacher near the front of the room	Special and general education classroom			9/23/22
Copy of class notes	As needed	Special and general education classroom			9/23/22
Extended time for assessments	As needed	Special and general education classroom	As needed	During assessments	9/23/22

Liberty Academic School
XXXX XXXX XXXXXX
XXXXXXX XXXXXX
XXXXXXX XXXXXX
Telephone: XXXXXX
Fax: XXXXXXXXXX
Email: xxxxx@xxxx.com
Website: www.xxxxxxx.com

Individual Education Program
Related Services

	Related Services					
Service	Service Delivery Recommendations	Person Responsible	Instructional Setting	Frequency	Duration	Services Begin
Speech/ Language Therapy	Small group (5:1)	Mr. Greer	Therapy room	Twice weekly	40 mins	Beginning 10/19/22
~ Identify, if applicable, class size, language (if other than English), group or individual services, direct and/or indirect consultant teacher services, or other service delivery recommendations.						

12-Month Service and/or Program					
Student is eligible to receive special education services and/or program during July/August: Yes or No (circle one) If yes, ______ Student will receive the same special education program/services as recommended above. OR ______ Student will receive the following special education program/services:					
Special Education Program/Services	**Service Delivery Recommendations**	**Instructional Setting**	**Frequency**	**Duration**	**Services Begin**

Liberty Academic School
XXXX XXXX XXXXXX
XXXXXXX XXXXXX
XXXXXXX XXXXXX
Telephone: XXXXXX
Fax: XXXXXXXXXX
Email: xxxxx@xxxx.com
Website: www.xxxxxxx.com

Individualized Education Plan
Assessments

Individual testing accommodations, specific to the student's disability and needs, to be used consistently by the student in the recommended educational program and in the administration of district-wide assessments of the student achievement and, in accordance with department policy, state assessments of student achievement as indicated below.

______ No testing accommodations are recommended OR

Testing Accommodation	Condition	Implementation Recommendations
Describe the type, length, and purpose of the test upon which the use of testing accommodations is conditioned, if applicable. Identify the amount of extended time, type of setting, etc., specific to testing accommodations, if applicable.		
• Time and a half extended time • Administered in special education classroom • Use of a computer	For all quizzes/tests: Read aloud to student Use of computer	Tests administered in a small group (3-5 students) Computer used to read to the student and/or to type answers

Narrative Explanation of Assessment Decision
Due to Brett's specific learning disability, he is given extended time on assignments and tests. He is easily distracted and thus will benefit from being away from distractions and allowed to complete assignments and tests with a small group of students or in a one-on-one setting. The use of computer aides with specially designed instruction such as web-based instructions and the use of earphones, will be allowed.

Participation in State and District-wide Assessments

__✓__ The student will participate in the same state and district-wide assessments administered to the general education students.

______ The student will participate in an alternate assessment on a state or district-wide assessment of student achievement. If checked, identify the alternate assessment below.

____
Alternate Assessment

Note the reason the student will not participate in the same state and district-wide assessments administered to the general education students and why the specific alternative assessment is appropriate.

Liberty Academic School
XXXX XXXX XXXXXX
XXXXXXX XXXXXX
XXXXXXX XXXXXX
Telephone: XXXXXX
Fax: XXXXXXXXXX
Email: xxxxx@xxxx.com
Website: www.xxxxxxx.com

Individualized Education Plan
Transition Plan Cover Page

Student Name: Brett Smith Date: 9/6/22

Disability: Intellectual Disability

Grade: 9th DOB: 3/24/07 Age: 15

Parent/Guardian Name: David & Mary Smith

Street Address: 1101 First Street

City: Majestic State: VA Zip Code: 12345

Phone #: 123-456-7890

A copy of the IEP was given to the parent/guardian/student on: 9/7/18

IEP Team Leader: Kelly Garman Phone #: 111-111-1111

The Individualized Education Plan (IEP) that accompanies this document is meant to support the team approach to ensuring successful outcomes for the student. The IEP is a working document that outlines the student's strengths, needs, and vision for the future. The intent of an IEP is to bring together a team of people who understand and support the student in order to come to a consensus on a transition plan that is appropriate and effective for the student.

Important Details to Document	Date
Transition IEP will be reviewed no later than	7/19/22
Parent notified of Transition Plan IEP Meeting	9/6/22
Student notified of Transition Plan IEP Meeting (if applicable)	N/A
Transition Plan IEP Meeting	9/20/22
Most recent eligibility date	2/15/22
Next Re-evaluation, including eligibility, must occur before	7/19/24

Participants Involved

The list below indicates that the individual participated in the development of the IEP and the decisions regarding placement. Participation does not authorize consent. Parent consent (or student if 18+) is indicated on the "Prior Notice" page.

Name of Participant	Position
David & Mary Smith	Father and Mother
Brett Smith	Student
Shonda Miller	Administrator
Kelly Garman	Special Education Teacher, Team Leader
Stuart Fisher	General Education Teacher
Dr. Nathaniel Salinas	Guidance Counselor
Russ Greer	Speech-language Therapist

Individualized Education Plan
Transition Cover Page, continued

The parent and student must be notified at least one year prior to the student turning 18 that the IDEA procedural safeguards will transfer to the student at the age of 18. This notice must be accompanied by an explanation of those procedural safeguards. If applicable, sign below documenting notification.

Parent Signature: ______________________________

Student Signature: ______________________________

Date informed: 9/20/22

IEP Team Member or Administrator Signature: Kelly Garman

Diploma and Transition Status

Projected Graduation Date: May, 2026

Is the student projected to graduate/exit this school year? Yes or (No) (circle one)
If yes, inform the parents and student that a *Summary of Performance* will be provided prior to graduating/exiting school.

Will the student be graduating with a standard, technical, or higher-level diploma or exceeding the age of eligibility this year? Yes or (No) (circle one)
If yes, a *Summary of Performance* must be provided to the student prior to graduating or exceeding the age of eligibility.

This student is a candidate for:	
______ Advanced Studies Diploma	______ Modified Standard Diploma
______ Advanced Technical Diploma	______ Special Diploma
__✓__ Standard Diploma	______ Certificate of Completion Program
______ Technical Diploma	______ General Education Diploma
______ General Achievement Diploma	______ Not discussed at this time

Liberty Academic School
XXXX XXXX XXXXXX
XXXXXXX XXXXXX
XXXXXXX XXXXXX
Telephone: XXXXXX
Fax: XXXXXXXXXX
Email: xxxxx@xxxx.com
Website: www.xxxxxxx.com

Individualized Education Plan
Transition Plan

Transition plans should begin no later than when the student is 16 years of age, or earlier if required by state law or if deemed necessary by the IEP team. The plan for transition services must be discussed and documented annually.

Student Name: Brett Smith Age: 14

Date Form Completed: ____________

Anticipated Graduation Date: May, 2026

Current IEP Dates from: 9/20/22 to: 9/20/23

Post-Secondary Goal

In the box below, write the student's post-secondary goal. This goal should be written in collaboration with the IEP team including the family and student. Include preferences, interests, and desired outcomes for post-secondary education, training, employment, and adult living.

Brett's goal is to attend vocational training and earn his certification as an auto-mechanic. He wishes to work at his neighbor's auto repair shop as a mechanic. He intends to live independently.

In the box below, write the disability-related skills that require IEP goals and/or related services. Consider all disability-related skills necessary for the student to achieve the stated post-secondary vision noted above.

In consideration of the present levels of performance, transition service needs of the student focus on the student's courses of study, taking into account the student's strengths, preferences, and interests as they relate to transition from school to post-school activities. Brett needs to further develop work-related skills and self-advocacy skills. He will complete the necessary coursework required for graduation with a Liberty Academic High School standard diploma. He needs to develop skills that will allow him to live independently, however, these skills are taught in the 10th and 11th grade curriculum.

Individualized Education Plan
Transition Plan, continued

Transition Plan Activities		
Needed Activities to Facilitate the Student's Movement from School to Post-School Activities	**Service/Activity**	**School/District/Agency Responsible**
Instruction	~ Review high school course syllabi for class preferences, with a focus on courses/electives in auto mechanics ~ Participate in general education elective courses and notify teachers of accommodations/modifications ~ Participate in IEP meetings and communicate personal accommodations, assist in the development of goals, and articulate personal modifications needed in an educational setting ~ Manage time schedules for daily and long-term assignments/projects	~ Student, parent, guidance counselor ~ Student, general education teacher, special education teacher ~ Student, parent, general education teacher, special education teacher, guidance counselor, psychologist ~ Student, special education teacher
Related Services	Speech/Language Therapy to improve communication skills	~ Student, Speech/Language Therapist
Community Experiences	Participate in community service activities/internship through auto mechanics course	~ Student, general education teacher
Development of Employment and other Post-High School Adult Living Objectives	Create a profile on Career Zone to research and further refine career preferences in auto mechanics	~ Student, special education teacher, guidance counselor
Daily Living Skills (if applicable)	Considering Brett's current levels of performance, Daily Living Skills (DLS) is not needed at this time	N/A
Functional Vocational Assessment (if applicable)	Considering Brett's current levels of performance, Functional Vocational Assessment (FVA) is not needed at this time	N/A

Liberty Academic School

XXXX XXXX XXXXXX
XXXXXXX XXXXXX
XXXXXXX XXXXXX

Telephone: XXXXXX
Fax: XXXXXXXXXX
Email: xxxxx@xxxx.com
Website: www.xxxxxxx.com

Individualized Education Plan
Prior Notice and Parental Consent

Student Name: Brett Smith

Meeting Details:

IEP Meeting Date: 9/20/22

Meeting Time: 1:30

Meeting Location: D221

Please complete and return this form to:

Kelly Garman	Kgarman@email.com	(111)-111-1111
Team Leader	Email	Phone Number

This document serves as notice prior to implementing this IEP. The decisions made in this IEP are based on a review of the students Present Levels of Academic and Functional Achievement. Relevant documentation to these decisions, if any, are attached. If you need additional information or have concerns, please contact the team leader.

Parent/Adult Student Consent: Indicate your decision by checking the appropriate space below and sign.

_✓_ I GIVE permission to implement this IEP.

____ I DO NOT GIVE permission to implement this IEP.

David Smith — 9/20/22

Parent or Adult Student Signature — Date

Transfer of Rights at the Age of Majority (age 18)

Indicate the date that the student and parent were informed of the transfer of parental rights under IDEA to the adult student at the age of 18. This must occur at least one year prior to the student turning 18 years of age.

I was informed of the parental rights under IDEA and that these rights transfer to me at age 18.

____________________ ________

Adult Student Signature — Date

I was informed of the parental rights under IDEA that transfer to my child at age 18.

____________________ ________

Parent Signature — Date

Functional Behavior Assessment Summary

Student: Brett Smith DOB: 3/24/07
School: Liberty Academic School Grade: 9th
Date: 9/27/22 Assessor: Kelly Garman

Data Sources:

- ☑ Observations (settings: classroom, lunchroom)
- ☑ Teacher interview
- ☑ Student interview
- ☑ Parent contact
- ☐ Other______________

Description of Target Behaviors:

Noncompliant and disruptive behavior: Brett does not often comply with teacher directions or classroom rules. He is oftentimes disruptive to the learning environment by calling out and being out of his seat. Brett does not always stop the inappropriate behavior when he is told to stop. At times, he has demonstrated argumentative behavior with the teacher. Brett has an active body and has a hard time sitting still and remaining on task. He rocks back and forth and bounces, and he is frequently fiddling with a pencil sharpener during class time. He requires multiple prompts to stay on task and becomes very easily distracted by things around him and things in his desk.

Lacks appropriate social interactions: Brett also has trouble engaging appropriately and positively with his classmates. He often misjudges the intentions of others, and his efforts to interact playfully are not always effective.

Frequency of Behaviors:

Brett's behaviors occur daily and can vary depending on events that occurred prior to him entering the classroom. Specific tasks that are challenging to Brett, such as reading and worksheets, can also trigger negative responses from him.

Duration of Behaviors:

Depending on the response to Brett's behavior, escalation can occur, or Brett can be redirected at times. If Brett's behavior escalates, he can demonstrate and engage in negative behaviors for an entire class period.

Intensity:

There are two major impacts of Brett's behavior. First, Brett's negative behaviors and off-task behaviors can often times keep him from learning. Second, Brett also expressed that he has trouble-making friends, and his negative classroom behaviors have made establishing and maintaining friendships more difficult.

Setting:

Brett has struggled and expressed frustration in a variety of settings. Socially, he has difficulty in unstructured settings such as physical education (PE), recess, lunch, and the bathroom. Academically, he struggles in the classroom to sit still and conform to expectations. Brett has demonstrated challenging behaviors in all settings throughout the school day.

Triggers:

Directing Brett to complete written work can be a trigger. Writing is challenging for him. If Brett has to sit quietly, he will likely struggle to keep his body still. Public correction may also be a trigger for negative behavior.

Brett also appears to have great difficulty keeping himself focused and quiet when the class is reviewing work that he already understands. He works at a faster pace than most of his classmates, and because he "check out" when other students need extra explanation, he gets caught up in distracting activities such as talking, fiddling in his desk, and moving around.

Working beyond 8 to 10 min will likely trigger off task behavior for Brett. His maximum work span and attention span are about 10 min. Beyond that negative distracting behaviors are triggered.

Consequences:

For the most part, Brett's behavior is being ignored in the classroom when possible. He is being redirected to appropriate behaviors when doing so results in minimal distraction to other students. Brett has been sent to the assistant principal to discuss his behavior when his behavior has become extreme and disruptive to the learning process of other students.

Educational Impact:

Brett's behavior is preventing him from engaging fully in the learning process. His behavior also distracts his classmates from fully engaging in the learning process.

Strengths/Resources

Student:

Brett can be very honest at times. He can admit when he makes a mistake when he is given some time to process the situation.

Brett has demonstrated the ability to hold himself accountable for his own actions despite his tendency to blame others for causing the initial problem.

Brett participates readily and actively in morning and afternoon check-in as part of his daily experiences at school. He is always willing to work on a new goal and he is honest about acknowledging when he cannot meet his goal or did not try his hardest.

School:

Brett receives services under an IEP as a student with attention deficit hyperactivity disorder. He is placed in a co-taught classroom and receives a lot of cueing and support from the special education teacher.

Brett meets regularly with the school psychologist for short check-in and regular processing sessions after an incident and he has been demonstrating honest and positive affect in his sessions.

Family:

Brett's mother is very supportive of her son and recognizes that he struggles with making good choices and that social skills are not a strength for him. She openly communicates with the school and has been supportive of efforts to support her son.

Community:

Brett sees an outside counselor on a regular basis. His mom picks him up from school to take him. At this time, the counseling experience is reported to be positive and somewhat helpful.

Function of the Student's Behavior:

- [x] To regulate affect (i.e., anxiety, anger, depression, lack of self-esteem)
- [x] To gain attention
- [ ] To gain control
- [x] To avoid/escape settings, tasks, individuals, situations
- [ ] To obtain specific object or activities
- [ ] To avoid/escape internal distractions (psychological/physical/neurological difficulties)
- [ ] To communicate needs or desires (lacks effective communication skills)
- [ ] Other ___________

Observational Data:

Brett was observed in his language arts class. When given a motivator to finish his quiz and earn iPad time, he worked steadily for 8 min. He turned in the quiz and waited patiently for the iPad to be given to him. He was told he needed to wait by his teacher, and he coped with the delayed gratification and was able to sit fairly quietly. He put his head down for a couple of minutes, and then began fiddling with a pencil sharpener. He did remain in his seat and was mostly quiet.

During the next part of the observation, Brett was expected to sit and listen to instructions on the country project that his class was working on. He was able to stay seated and once the kids were given the go-ahead to start working, Brett was allowed to earn his iPad time. He transitioned from the iPad and began working on his project without incident. He was eager to start on his poster like many of the other students, but he had not collected his facts yet and was a bit behind. It was hard for him to not work on the hands on portion of the project, but his teacher directed him to go back to his seat and finish finding his facts. He insisted he had found them, and she told him to go to his seat and raise his hand and wait for her to come check it like she did with all the other students. Brett complied and went back to his seat and raised his hand. The teacher finished working with another student, and then came to Brett. She gave him some feedback and required him to gather a little more information. Brett did not appear to get upset. He went back to the computer to look for more facts.

In math class, Brett was able to compute math facts quickly. His brain works quicker than his ability to record his processing. Brett expressed this to the Observer. He may benefit from some self-paced math on a computer where he can be challenged at his level and work speed that keeps him engaged and learning.

Brett often draws pictures when he is upset. He does a good job of choosing colors that represent his mood. Most of his drawings show a combination of different colors that represent emotions. Anger is most often included, along with sad. He will frequently include small sections of green to indicate happy and sometimes other colors, such as orange and yellow, to indicate some struggle. Brett seems to demonstrate feeling better after he draws.

Brett was observed having a facilitated interaction with a peer. The other student was asked to provide some feedback to Brett. =The student shared honestly that he feels kids would like to be friends with Brett but when he does not follow the rules, or he is disrespectful to the teacher, he is going to be judged more negatively. Brett was asked how he feels about the student. He replied, "I like him because he is nice, but I don't like him because he's not my friend." Brett became emotional when he later admitted that he has a lot of trouble making friends.

Hypothesis Statement:

Brett has a hard time keeping his body still. He also does not always make appropriate choices. His motivation for misbehavior seems to be driven to get attention or avoid nonpreferred tasks. Brett needs to stay engaged and kept busy. He computes math in his head and has a hard time slowing down his brain enough to show his work. It is difficult for him to wait while others are still processing the information that comes easily to him.

Brett's fine motor skills are poor based on work samples. His writing mechanics are not at grade level. His writing content appears to be good, but he lacks organizational skills. Brett may produce more work if he uses speech-to-text on assignments and assessments that are not assessing the skill of writing.

Graphic organizers would be very useful in helping Brett organize thoughts and navigate him through the writing process.

Brett frequently seeks attention in a negative way. He admits it and recognizes it later. Brett processes extremely well and has been able to be honest.

Brett's efforts to make friends and connect with peers are frequently the wrong type of efforts. He tries to show off and to be silly, and he intentionally breaks the rules, but is not making the connection that these behaviors are not peer-approved and are causing him further isolation from social relationships.

Similarly, in the classroom, it appears that Brett is trying to impress his classmates, and he wants to be accepted. His misguided efforts keep him from making friends.

Brett's mix of emotions, lack of emotional control, and self-regulation make it a challenging mix of feelings that results in challenging behaviors. This oftentimes results in poor behavioral choices and outbursts.

Suggested Recommendation/Replacement Behavior(s):

Provided scheduled breaks for Brett during the day and structuring his work with a numbered list of goals may increase his overall motivation and work production. This model should be coupled with motivators that he can earn from a list of options.

Brett is highly motivated by a ticket system where the teacher sends home positive notes to his parents to reward his efforts. He is able to process honesty and can admit when he has not earned a privilege.

Brett needs to learn to employ some coping strategies such as writing about his feelings in a feelings journal or drawing a picture if he is not feeling well. Oftentimes, when Brett has an opportunity to express how he is feeling in words or pictures, he is able to "move on," and make better choices. He responds very well to specific guidance and directions.

Brett's "infractions: need to be processed within in a neutral environment when he is calm. A tracking sheet of negative behavior choices may be helpful to assist him in recognizing where he made a poor choice. Providing positive choices as an alternative may help him to choose wisely the next time.

Morning check-ins are recommended to help identify Brett's mood and set a behavioral goal for the day. Brett may need to have scheduled breaks throughout the day if his behavior begins to decline. Building in breaks after 10 min of work may allow Brett the time he needs to move which should allow him to reset so that he can begin to work again.

Use of a timer or stopwatch to help Brett use his time more efficiently.

Use of a prompt counting card to help Brett keep track of his prompts during the day and try to earn independent work time credits may help him keep this as a goal and track his progress. Simple index card with tally marks should be sufficient.

Blended learning style is recommended so that he may be challenged.

Asking Brett to restate the expectations and demonstrate them may be more effective than a reprimand or verbal correction.

Positive Behavior Supports Attempted:

Earning "stars" for good behavior (PBIS)
Sending to the assistant principal
Ignoring the behavior
Parent contact
Staff meeting with parents
Discussion
Warnings

Behavior Intervention Plan

Student: Brett Smith **DOB:** 3/24/07

School: Liberty Academic School **Grade:** 9th

Date: 9/27/22 **Case Manager:** Kelly Garman

Goal for Plan:
Brett will maintain safety 100% of the time across school settings during the first marking period (9/28/22–1/22/22) by accessing/utilizing strategies and supports for self-regulation during challenging moments.
Brett will complete 100% of classroom tasks with a compliance rate of 85% during the first marking period (9/28/22–1/22/22).

Setting Events, Triggers, Contexts (Antecedents):
Competitive games/activities
Unstructured social situations (i.e., Physical education (PE), recess, lunch, bus, transitions, bathroom)
Extended work periods (greater than 8–10 min)
Extended writing assignments
Idle wait time

Hypothetical Function of Behaviors (per FBA 9/27/22):
To gain attention
To avoid/escape settings, tasks, individuals, or situations
To regulate affect

Behavior Intervention Plan

Noncompliance	**Prevention:** • Agree on nonverbal cues between Brett and the teacher for self-advocacy when he needs or wants something • Provide access for typing when lengthier written work is required (more than one paragraph) • Schedule noncontingent breaks • Provide verbal checks to help him use time efficiently • Give motivators tied to task compliance and completion **Consequence:** • Give a direction • If student in noncompliant, repeat directions • If still noncompliant, repeat directions again and remind Brett of possible reinforcers if he complies • If still noncompliant, offer choices or alternatives and continue this process three times • After three attempts, give space and ignore as long as no safety issues arise • Attempt to reengage following next natural transition that occurs **Follow-up:** • Process all behaviors in a private, neutral setting once he has regained focus and calmed down • Utilize restorative questioning sheets to guide the discussion

Argumentative Behaviors	**Prevention:**
	• Avoid public correction
	• Create a safe space for Brett to retreat to without seeking permission to avoid engaging in argumentative behaviors
	• Record stressors
	• Monitor negative self-talk
	• Teach how to disagree appropriately
	    • "I" statements
	    • Draw it
	    • Write a complaint letter
	• Acknowledge his "power," but remind him no one is obligated to argue for him
	    • No one wins anything by arguing or giving in, but most of us argue and eventually give in
	    • Conflict motivators (rewards)
	    • Control/change your role in these moments
	• Praise his ambition and redirect to something more useful
	• Try to achieve mutual understanding
	Consequences:
	• Point out when Brett is arguing: "I feel like you are arguing with me. I need you to be flexible"
	• Encourage him to stop, stay calm, and make a new plan

	• Use one of the following strategies:
	    • "I statements"
	    • Draw it
	    • Write a letter of complaint
	• If arguing continues, acknowledge Brett's "power," but remind him no one is obligated to argue with him. Use statements such as:
	    • No one wins anything by arguing or giving in, but most of us argue and eventually give in. Think about what you want to control now. This conflict seems motivated by your opinions, interests, goals, desire to gain power, status, or something else. Let us discuss what you want or need
	• Praise Brett's ambition and redirect to something more useful that would not embarrass him in front of his peers
	• Try to find mutual understanding

Social Skills	**Prevention:** • Give a prompt regarding upcoming social skills requirements or situation that may cause him stress • Model expectations for group work • Allow Brett to observe activities prior to engaging • Try to explain the intention of others • Allow Brett to work independently unless someone is available to supervise the group • Use social skills scripts and social stories • Provide a limited number of social escape cards per day to allow Brett to leave an uncomfortable situation. • Pair/group students strategically for success • Separate from triggering classmates

	Consequences: • Review social stories • Role play or practice social skills needed in isolation with the school counselor or teacher • Repeat this as many times as possible to help solidify the skill

Hyperactivity/ Impulsivity	**Prevention:** • Ignore rocking, bouncing, and fidgeting that does not interfere with learning • Provide extra space for Brett to move without touching or distracting others • Avoid unstructured time • Allowed structured exercise breaks every 20 min • Provide access to sensory tool kit • Consider allowing wiggle seat, fidget band on chair, weighted lap pad during seat work • Display visual reminders of work area (boundary markers) **Consequences:** • If hyperactive/impulsive behaviors are harmful, inconsiderate, or disrespectful, they should be addressed using restorative processing in a private setting to identify triggers and ways for Brett to manage his body and mind

Interventions:	**Person(s) Responsible for Implementing Intervention:**

• **Check-in/Check-out (Social-Emotional)**
  • Check-in with classroom teacher in the morning
  • Check-outs with homeroom teacher before leaving, including reflection on positive behavior and goals sent home daily
  • Breaks requested throughout the day
	• **Check-in/Check-out (Social-Emotional)**
	  • School social worker/psychologist, special educator, general education teacher

• **Social Skills Training**
  • Access to and review of social stories
  • Planned, noncompetitive recess opportunities
  • Access to appropriate coping strategies
	• **Social Skills Training**
	  • School social worker/psychologist to provide stories, help with development of recess activities, develop coping strategies
	  • Teacher will assist with access and encouragement

• **Classroom Accommodations**
  • Access to bulleted list outlining expectations for each of his daily activities
  • Preset verbal expectations in "I need you to…" rather than, "do not…"
  • Access to coping strategies and tools
  • Preferential seating
  • Utilization of appropriate preventative and consequence techniques including referral when necessary
  • Proximity to teacher
	• **Classroom Accommodations**
	  • Teacher and special educator

• Graphic organizers • Assignments broken down into smaller more manageable sizes • Check to ensure understanding of assignments • Oral discussion with teacher before writing assignment • Small group testing	
• **Daily Report Card/Token Economy** • Earned independent time and rewards for completing tasks and maintaining safety • Point system to communicate daily behaviors with family • Reflection on positive behaviors and goals for the next day	• **Daily Report Card/Token Economy** • Teachers will assign points throughout the day • Special educator/homeroom teacher will assist with positive reflection and goal for the next day • Rewards will be based on what student earns but may include mental health personnel, principal, assistant principal, teachers, or parents
• **Identification of Trusted Adult in Each Setting**	• **Identification of Trusted Adult in Each Setting** • Teachers

Review Date: ____________________

Signatures	**Role**
	Student
	Parent
	Administrator
	General Educator
	Special Educator
	Paraprofessional
	Mental Health Professional
	Other:
	Other:

Special Education Acronyms

Below is a list of commonly used acronyms pertaining to special education. Though we will try our best to use the full terms or offer an explanation as we proceed, please use these as a reference in case we inadvertently use acronyms in the meeting without an explanation.

AAC Alternative Augmentative Communication
ABA Applied Behavioral Analysis
ADA Americans with Disabilities Act
ADD/ADHD Attention Deficit/Attention Deficit Hyperactivity Disorder
APR Annual Performance Report
ASD Autism Spectrum Disorder
AT Assistive Technology
AYP Annual Yearly Progress
BIP Behavioral Intervention Plan
BOE Board of Education
CBA Curriculum-Based Assessment
CCSS Common Core State Standards
CEC Council for Exceptional Children
CST Child Study Program
DOE Department of Education
DSM Diagnostic and Statistical Manual of Mental Disorders
ED Emotional Disturbance
IEE Independent Educational Evaluation
EI Early Intervention
ELL English Language Learner
EIS Early Intervention Services
ELL English Language Learner
ESD Extended School Day
ESL English as a Second Language
ESSA Every Student Succeeds Act
ESYS Extended School Year Services
FAPE Free Appropriate Public Education
FBA Functional Behavior Assessment
FERPA Family Educational Rights and Privacy Act
FOIA Freedom of Information Act
IA Instructional Assistant
ID Intellectual Disabilities
IDEA Individuals with Disabilities Education Act
IEP Individualized Educational Plan
IFSP Individualized Family Service Plan
ITP Individualized Transition Plan
LD Learning Disability
LEA Local Education Agency
LEP Limited English Proficiency
LRE Least Restrictive Environment
MDR Manifestation Determination Review
NCLB No Child Left Behind Act (Reauthorized in 2015 as ESSA—Every Student Succeeds Act)
OCD Obsessive Compulsive Disorder
ODD Oppositional Defiant Disorder
OT Occupational Therapy
PALS Peer-Assisted Learning System
PBS Positive Behavior Supports
PD Physical Disability
PDD Pervasive Developmental Disorder
PLAAFP Present Levels of Academic Achievement and Functional Performance
PLEP Present level of performance
RTI Response to Intervention
SE Special Education
SED Serious Emotional Disturbance
SI Sensory Integration
SLD Specific Learning Disability
SLI Speech Language Impairment
SLP Speech/Language Pathologist
SST Student Study Team
Voc Ed Vocational Education
VR Vocational Rehabilitation

Bible Verses Used in Each Chapter

Scripture references throughout the book are from the New International Version Bible unless otherwise indicated.

Chapter 1

"I will lead the blind by a way they do not know, in paths they do not know I will guide them. I will make darkness into light before them and rugged places into plains. These are the things I will do, And I will not leave them undone," Isaiah 42:16 (New American Standard Bible).

"Let everyone be subject to the governing authorities, for there is no authority except that which God has established. The authorities that exist have been established by God," Romans 13:1.

"Do nothing through rivalry or through conceit, but in humility, each counting others better than himself," Philippians 2:3 (World English Bible).

"For you created my inmost being; you knit me together in my mother's womb. I praise you because I am fearfully and wonderfully made; your works are wonderful, I know that full well. My frame was not hidden from you when I was made in the secret place, when I was woven together in the depths of the earth. Your eyes saw my unformed body; all the days ordained for me were written in your book before one of them came to be," Psalm 139:13–16.

Chapter 2

"Do not think of yourself more highly then you ought, but rather think of yourself with sober judgment, in accordance with the faith God has distributed to each of you. For just as each of us has one body with many members, and these members do not all have the same function," Romans 12:3b-4.

"Speak out on behalf of the voiceless, and for the rights of all who are vulnerable," Proverbs 31:8 (Common English Bible).

Chapter 3

"By wisdom the LORD laid the earth's foundations, by understanding he set the heavens in place," Proverbs 3:19.

As Christians, we are taught in the Bible that wisdom and understanding come from the Lord

- "I have filled him with the Spirit of God, with wisdom, with understanding, with knowledge and with all kinds of skills," Exodus 31:3.
- "God gave Solomon wisdom and very great insight, and a breadth of understanding as measureless as the sand on the seashore," 1 Kings 4:29.
- "The whole world sought audience with Solomon to hear the wisdom God had put in his heart," 1 Kings 10:24.

"The rain came down, the streams rose, and the winds blew and beat against that house; yet it did not fall, because it had its foundation on the rock," Matthew 7:25.

"But the one who hears my words and does not put them into practice is like a man who built a house on the ground without a foundation. The moment the torrent struck that house, it collapsed and its destruction was complete," Luke 6:49.

Chapter 4

"For I know the plans I have for you," declares the Lord, "plans to prosper you and not to harm you, plans to give you hope and a future," Jeremiah 29:11.

"Commit to the Lord whatever you do, and he will establish your plans," Proverbs 16:3.

"Plans fail for lack of counsel, but with many advisers they succeed," Proverbs 15:22.

"For as in one body we have many members, and the members do not all have the same function, so we, though many, are one body in Christ, and individually members one of another. Having gifts that differ according to the grace given to us, let us use them," Romans 12:4–6 (English Standard Version).

"When pride comes, then comes disgrace, but with humility comes wisdom," Proverbs 11:2.

"Pride goes before destruction, a haughty spirit before a fall," Proverbs 16:18.

"Let us not become weary in doing good, for at the proper time we will reap a harvest if we do not give up," Galatians 6:9.

Chapter 5

"Rejoice always, pray continually, give thanks in all circumstances; for this is God's will for you in Christ Jesus," I Thess. 5:16–18.

"We also pray that you will be strengthened with all his glorious power so you will have all the endurance and patience you need. May you be filled with joy," Colossians 1:11 (New Living Translation).

"You shall not curse a deaf man nor place a stumbling block before the blind, but you shall revere your God; I am the LORD," Leviticus 19:14 (Amplified Bible).

"Therefore, let us not pass judgment on one another any longer, but rather decide never to put a stumbling block or hindrance in the way of a brother," Romans 14:13 (ESV).

Chapter 6

"You shall not curse a deaf man nor place a stumbling block before the blind, but you shall revere your God; I am the LORD," Leviticus 19:14 (Amplified Bible).

"Bear one another's burdens, and so fulfill the law of Christ," Galatians 6:2 (ESV).

Chapter 7

"To aspire to leadership is an honorable ambition," 1 Timothy 3:1.

"Not many of you should become teachers, my fellow believers, because you know that we who teach will be judged more strictly," James 3:1.

"I can do all things through Christ who gives me strength," Philippians 4:13.

Chapter 8

"Who is wise and understanding among you? Let them show it by their good life, by deeds done in the humility that comes from wisdom," James 3:13.

"Be always humble, gentle, and patient. Show your love by being tolerant with one another," Ephesians 4:2 (Good News Translation).

"Do not let kindness and truth leave you; Bind them around your neck, Write them on the tablet of your heart," Proverbs 3:3 (NASB).

"Let no corrupting talk come out of your mouths, but only such as is good for building up, as fits the occasion, that it may give grace to those who hear," Ephesians 4:29 (ESV).

"Rejoice in hope, be patient in tribulation, be constant in prayer," Romans 12:12.

"Therefore, if you have any encouragement from being united with Christ, if any comfort from his love, if any common sharing in the Spirit, if any tenderness and compassion, then make my joy complete by being like-minded, having the same love, being one in spirit and of one mind. Do nothing out of selfish ambition or vain conceit. Rather, in humility value others above yourselves, not looking to your own interests but each of you to the interests of the others," Philippians 2:1–4.

"For just as each of us had one body with many members, and these members do not all have the same function, so in Christ we, though many, form one body, and each member belongs to all the others. We have different gifts, according to the grace given to each of us. If your gift is prophesying, then prophesy in accordance with your faith; if it is serving, then serve; if it is teaching, then teach; if it is to encourage, then give encouragement; if it is giving, then give generously; if it is to lead, do it diligently; if it is to show mercy, do it cheerfully," Romans 12:4–8.

"The Lord make his face shine upon you and be gracious to you; the Lord turn his face toward you and give you peace," Numbers 6:25–26.